QUADRUPLETS

A Love Story

JANNA WAGNER

www.magwagpress.com, quads@magwagpress.com

Published by MagWag Press
San Diego, California

Printed and bound in the United States of America

ISBN: 979-8-9850362-0-6

DEDICATION

I dedicate this book to my husband Larry—my best friend, lover, and father of our children.

Contents

PROLOGUE

Some stories need to be told before they're lost forever.

This is one of them.

PART ONE

1

THE DOMINO EFFECT

I'm absolutely spent, and can hardly wait to get home, drop my duffel bag, and throw myself on the bed. The trip back to Seattle to visit family and friends was great. But the return trip included a flight change, a layover, shuttles, and finally a bus ride home to my college town in California.

It feels good to be back in sunny San Diego, returning to college life and my rented house with Lorena and Cassandra, my two roommates. Lorena is skinny, fairly spunky, and she doesn't have a problem speaking her mind. Cassandra is just about the opposite ... plump, soft-spoken, and always smiling. We three are best friends, so we do everything together—food, movies, amusement parks, you name it. I wonder what we'll do together tonight after I get a quick snooze and a shower.

As I enter the house, something doesn't feel quite right. I'm hearing muffled voices coming from ... where? Setting my duffel bag down, I push a strand of blond hair behind my right ear. Standing there for a moment, I listen for the muffled voices again. I follow the sound. It leads me to the converted garage, which serves as my flute-teaching studio in the front and my bedroom in the back. The two halves are separated by a curtain. I tiptoe slowly and cautiously down the hallway, like a cat caught in a bout of curiosity, until I'm standing outside my room, listening to the voices on the other side of my door. It goes silent. *Maybe they are going to surprise me with a big welcome home.* My lip curls up a bit into an "I got ya" smile. *Maybe I should go outside and around the house. I can throw the door open from the other side and hear them let out a surprised shriek.* But I pause. *And spoil their fun? Never!* I start to open the door as if I haven't heard anything.

Something seems to be telling me to wait. But it's been almost two weeks, and I'm excited to see my friends again. I put my hand on the knob and turn. As the door opens, I throw open the curtain. My eyes widen as my jaw drops, and I suck down way too much air as my heart begins to race. I can't believe it. There in the bed is Cassandra and my boyfriend Michael, wrapped in each other's arms. Have I been blind? Stealing each other's boyfriends is not something best friends do. *What about Michael—what changed? We both agreed on saving intimacy for marriage.*

"Please, baby, it's not what … we were … I just …," Michael blurts out.

"I'm so sorry, Janna," Cassandra says.

I shout: "I can't believe you two could do this to me!" *I'm shocked and crushed. How can this be happening?* Running through the house, I stop just long enough to grab the duffel bag I'd left near the main entrance and walk out. This is the first domino that falls.

◆　◆　◆　◆

I stomp around to the back of the house, then to the curb where I'd parked my car before leaving for Seattle ten days ago—I'm staring at an empty space where the car used to be. *Who would even want to steal my old Renault? It always had to be pushed down the sloping street daily for a jump start. There's no way I am going to go back into the house to use the phone.* Across the street, I find a pay phone and call the police.

After I get to the right person I hear, "Miss Magnuson, Janna?"

"Yes, that's me."

"Your car has not been stolen, Miss Magnuson. I'm afraid it's been towed. You can get it back for a fine of $500." She pauses—there is an awkward silence as my mouth gapes open. She continues, "You just can't leave a car parked on the street longer than 48 hours."

"Keep it," I say. "I don't have five hundred dollars."

The second domino just fell.

◆ ◆ ◆ ◆

With all my gear in tow, I walk the ten blocks to San Diego State University (SDSU) to pick up my financial aid check. I get in line just before they announce that the office will close in five minutes. Standing in line, I'm barely able to push back tears and embarrassment. Hopelessness is becoming my new best friend. Finally, I reach the front.

"I'm sorry," the woman behind the counter says, "but your financial aid has been canceled." Her hazel eyes soften as she tilts her head to the side.

"Why?" I ask, choking on the word.

"You signed on the wrong line, see?" She directs my attention toward the document, then points to the correct line, moving up a bit to the incorrect place where I had signed.

"Oh," I whisper, after swallowing hard. *At least this bearer of bad news delivered it kindly.*

"God help me!" I mutter as I look up. The thought hits me: *I should have asked my parents for money*, but pride and shame have always been my natural deterrents to common sense.

The third domino just fell.

NO MORE GAMES

At 24, I'm making plans to complete my senior solo recital in *Flute Performance* at SDSU. That will complete my diploma path and allow me to get out of here. I'm eager to finish up, move back to Seattle, and start auditioning for orchestras. I'll also need to develop a flute-student clientele.

Something's not feeling right, I think. *Why am I so tired all the time? I get exhausted just walking across campus, and it's getting harder to play my flute too. I've been procrastinating for a while now, maybe it's time to visit the Student Health Services Department.*

As I walk away from health services, I shake my head in disbelief. I've never even heard of pleurisy, but it explains why it's difficult for me just to breathe, let alone play the flute.

I'm so close to graduation, I've got to figure a way to tough it out with this illness, I determine.

At my next doctor visit, he says, "Janna, if you continue to play the flute and continue to pursue your goal right now, it could kill you." Devastated, I fall into a deep depression, nearly completely broken.

Concerned about my depression, Steven, a fellow musician and a violinist I'd played duets with frequently, invites me to spend the weekend with his family, and I accept.

The ride to Escondido takes about an hour and is very relaxing. It feels like we're driving out into the country. As we pull into the driveway, Steven's mom comes out with a warm, welcoming smile. It's feeling like a safe place right now. I can tell by her tone as she greets us that she cares about people. Her kindness is disarming and I lower my guard a bit.

After a very deep sleep and a magnificent breakfast, we drive to their church. I agreed to go but I'm feeling a bit vulnerable. The size of the church is amazing—a megachurch. I've heard about these places, and my mind puts me on the defensive. *I don't want to fall for any hocus-pocus-faith stuff. I've seen enough of that in my teenage years and just don't trust preachers at all anymore.*

Sitting between Steven and his mom, we settle into comfortable balcony seats. I smile, I am polite, and I am agreeable—for her sake—but I am very cautious about accepting everything that I hear. As the service winds down, my heart softens a bit, and I feel a bit of a yearning. *I want to believe that this is a safe place and that I can let down my defenses.*

Still, my guard remains up. The man in the pulpit is asking us to pray. It couldn't hurt. So again, I'll be agreeable, but I'm keeping my eyes open.

Finally, the preacher says some familiar words, "You can have peace, belonging, and purpose if you turn your heart to Jesus."

I've heard that before and have always resisted deciding on the matter.

Hey, things couldn't get much worse for me. Maybe I should just give in and see how things go. Unexpectedly, I feel something happening in me. But I'm not about to give my friend Steven the satisfaction of thinking he's converted me or something, so I keep it to myself.

Overall, it's been a very relaxing weekend. I am grateful for Steven and his mom. I say my thank-yous to her, and we head back down to SDSU. The hospitality and going to their church weren't so painful after all, but this will be the end of it. *I'll never give Steven the satisfaction of thinking it had an impact on me.*

But, as the days go by, I can't help but recognize I'm at the end of myself. By opening my heart and mind, I do feel different about things. I feel peace, and I even feel loved, regardless of my circumstances. Maybe there *is* something more to that church and the family visit I had with Steven and his mom three weeks ago.

2

THE PRACTICE DUNGEON

Not graduating in the summer and waiting six months to get going again has been difficult. But like clockwork, the doctor's prediction of six months was spot-on. I've lost some of my flute chops, but they are returning quickly as I once again get ready for my senior flute performance.

The SDSU music department has an underground practice-room area. It's a lot like an underground garage, but without the cars. The offices and classrooms are upstairs. When I practice, I have to walk down two dark, steep, and unlit flights of concrete stairs to the basement. I feel my heart quicken as I look over my right and then left shoulder, to be sure no one is behind me. Perhaps I'm overly cautious, but I've been followed before, and I never want to repeat that experience. Clasping my flute case in my left hand, I open the unlocked door with my right. It's early Friday morning, 7:00 a.m., on this sunny day in the fall of 1976. I figure I'll have the place to myself. Sure enough, it's stone-cold quiet. Just me.

Clear to the end of the hallway, I enter my favorite cubbyhole. It's way at the back, near a water fountain. It's kind of creepy down here—at least for a female. I never really know who I might bump into. It's called the *dungeon* for a reason.

Each cubby is about eight feet wide and six feet deep. The door has a narrow glass window, so other students can check to see if it's occupied. Some cubbies have a piano, while some just have a music stand and a chair, for orchestral players like me, with my flute.

Inside, there is just barely enough room for me and my equipment. I always set up my stand facing away from the narrow window, so nothing will distract me. I place my sheet music on the stand and start practicing my scales followed by arpeggios, sometimes looking straight ahead at the wall, and sometimes closing my eyes, walking around with my flute, stepping to the rhythm of my playing. After pleurisy, I am incredibly grateful to be playing again, but even so, every day I have to motivate myself to put in the long six hours of practice. Not having started serious practice until my 20s, it was late to decide to become a flute performance major. Practicing these six hours a day is the only way that I can stay on par with my peers. It isn't always easy, but I tell myself that my weakness—not having a lot of years playing the flute—is also my strength. I am forced to discipline my mind with these sessions, in my determination to meet an almost impossible challenge. I'm forced to work hard, like it or not. In the process, I find ways to reward myself.

There is only one way I let myself out of practice. I bargain with myself. I tell myself that if I play for 15 minutes but I find I am still not into it, I can quit and just give it up for the day. But I've never exercised that option ... until today.

I just can't do this today, I tell myself. *I don't know what the problem is, but I'm going to pack up my flute and try this again later.*

Walking toward the front of the practice dungeon, I hear someone wailing away on the piano, doing some popular/rock kind of music, singing at the top of his lungs. *He must have come in at the other entrance after I'd already started practicing.* It's rare for the usual classical music kind of students who frequent the music department to play rock and to play that loud. As I peek into his little window, his back is to me. Suddenly, without warning, he jumps up, turns around, and opens the door, just as I'm pulling away from the window. Taken aback, not knowing what else to do, I put my hand in the air as if to say, "Hi."

All he does is smile, and I'm dazzled. He opens the door all the way and introduces himself as Larry. "Did you need this room?" he asks.

"I, uh … no. I just liked your …" Once again, this Larry guy has caught me off guard. "You just have a very nice voice."

"Thank you … uh …"

"Oh, I'm Janna."

"Pretty name. So, Janna … you sing also?"

"I play the flute."

"I think I've seen you before in some ensembles," he says. "Maybe accompanied by a classical guitar?"

I stumble on my thoughts for a moment, realizing that he's referring to Michael's group.

"Well, anyway, I've genuinely enjoyed your recitals. You have a great tone on flute, it really resonates."

Why do I feel like he's looking at my lips?

I blush. "Yeah, I guess. I mean, thank you."

"Besides playing the flute, what do you do for fun?"

"Well …" I can't believe it; my mind goes blank.

"I know I don't look it," he says, obviously detecting my nervousness, "but I'm kind of a motorcycle guy."

"I don't know anything about motorcycles."

"I can teach you a few things."

I grin.

Smooth. I wanted to know about the song he'd been singing. "What was that song you sang?"

"Oh, just a song I wrote."

"Wow, that's cool. It kind of sounded like it might be about God. … Was it about God?"

He hesitates, then I ask, "Are you a Christian?"

"Are you?" he asks. *Again, smooth.*

"Yes, I think I'm leaning that way," I respond without hesitation.

"Me too."

There is more small talk. Just as I open my mouth to say "Goodbye, maybe I'll see you again sometime," he says, "Perhaps I could accompany you to church this Sunday."

Perhaps I could accompany you to church?! Who says that?

I am a little skeptical but figure, how many guys would make such a request? He picks me up on his motorcycle, a Honda 90, which looks more like a bicycle than a motorcycle.

He had said something about also having a truck, so I wonder why he's choosing to pick me up on a motorcycle. *Is he gonna open up with the classic "Hold on tight"?* I ask myself. *Even though I am a bit reluctant to ride, there's no way he can put the moves on me, at least not without an audience.*

That date goes well. In fact, he wants me to meet his family. Although I'm not opposed to it, I'll put him on notice.

"You know," I say, "I'm going back to Seattle as soon as I complete my senior solo flute recital in a few weeks, six to be exact …"

"Is that set in stone?" he asks.

"Well, I'm not going to change my plans for anybody … unless it's for the man I'll marry."

He replies: "Perhaps I could help you with your recital programs and posting of your signs."

Oh, brother, what planet are you from? I think. Smoothly dodging questions by offering me irresistible favors.

I let him help me get ready for my recital. But my guard is way up, as if I have an impenetrable concrete wall all around me. It might not be fair, but I've been hurt before; I know it can happen again.

Did he completely miss my hint about "unless it's for the man I'll marry"? Or is he purposely dodging it? Is it chivalry? Is it the soft sell? Is it cowardice? Or is he just playing with my heart?

Larry helps me with my recital posters, and we fold programs together. He takes me to church again and out to eat a few times. On Halloween, we hit the haunted house in Balboa Park. The implication of his feelings is becoming obvious, and my heart softens. He doesn't seem to be able to speak straight-out about his feelings, but clearly, the warmth is amping up with each new experience we share.

As we walk into the haunted house, I'm spooked. *Maybe he thinks I'll be scared. I'll be scared, which is why when he puts his arm around me, I don't mind, even though I do feel like a bit of a sucker.* Smiling in the dark, I snuggle up to him. His gentle, low-risk overtures endear him to me.

SHOWTIME

It's the big recital day and it's going well, so far. I am honored that my parents drove 1,255 miles from Seattle to San Diego to be here. The violin, cello, and harpsichord players are all tuned up and in their places, ready for the curtains to open. Sherry, my harpsichord accompanist, gets up and walks silently over to the edge of the curtain to take a peek at the audience.

"It's a full house, Janna," she informs me. "You're going to do great and this is going to be maybe the best senior recital I've ever had the privilege of being a part of."

"Well, we have worked hard and are very well prepared," I say. "I think we deserve for this to be one of the best." I nod at her to hit "concert A" on the harpsichord again so that we can calibrate our pitch one last time. I smile at my fellow musicians and look over to the stagehand with a nod, signaling that he should open the red velvet floor-to-ceiling curtains now. As the curtain opens, the audience claps. With my sterling silver and gold custom-made and numbered Lamberson flute I walk to center stage and take a humble bow, catching a look at Larry, Mom, and Dad, who are seated dead center just a few rows back.

I'm ready for this and I want to enjoy the experience. I'm resolved not to let nerves spoil it. This will be sheer joy, I tell myself, as I walk back around to join the group, smiling at each of them along the way.

As I raise my flute to my lips, it signals the other musicians to raise their instruments to the ready position. I simultaneously take a deep breath, raise my chin slightly, and bring the flute down to signify the tempo and downbeat with that motion—and we're off. It is an exhilarating moment, and there is now nothing but this music in my reality. By some miracle, I am completely focused.

An hour later, Larry is the first to give me a standing ovation. It is a big deal that my parents are here. They grew up during the Great Depression, so frugality is their approach to money. This was why they weren't enthusiastic about my decision to become a music major—in their view, job prospects did not look promising.

The next day, Larry and I show them around San Diego. Mom pulls me aside as we enter the San Diego Automotive Museum and says, "We like him!"

Maybe a little too much, I think.

"Mom," I ask as we walk out of the museum. "Do you love me even half as much as you love this guy?"

"Of course I do, honey, but you already know I love you."

I get a little bit sulky once again, in a good way. I respect my parents' opinion, and if they like Larry, then I know he has to be someone special.

His Family

Within days I am meeting Larry's family. They live at the very north end of Palm Springs in an area called Windy Point. Greyhound busses and trucks have been known to turn over in the very strong winds that blow through. It's pretty much a desert backed by the huge 8,000-foot San Jacinto Mountains. There are a few houses in this place, but it's fairly barren ... beautiful but a little foreign to my Seattle senses.

As we approach the front door of his mom's very modest house, I'm nervous.

What if they don't like me? What if they think I'm not good enough for Larry?

These piranha thoughts keep swimming around my mind, threatening to nibble away at the bit of confidence I have. I've always prided myself on making good first impressions, and this one has to be spot-on.

Larry's mom is smiling from ear to ear. "Nice to meet you," she says, as she hugs me so tightly, and for so long, that I have to catch my breath after she pulls away. Still holding my shoulders, she gives me a big kiss right on the lips. Larry's brother Jon and sister Dani do the same, minus the kiss.

"Nice to meet you guys, too." I turn to Larry, "So you have two siblings, Larry?"

"Actually, I have another sister, Robbie, who lives in Michigan. I hope you'll meet her someday."

"What do you think?" Larry asks, looking at his family and then smirking at me. "Is she a keeper?"

"Anyone who gives you the time of day has got to be a keeper," his mom says, then winks at me.

Okay, I feel a little more at ease, but I'm still somewhat nervous. We gather in the family room—talk, eat snacks, and drink sodas.

I can see that all of them are humble and live in humble surroundings. I'm getting a warm feeling.

I soon learn that Tahquitz Canyon is part of Mt. San Jacinto, close to downtown Palm Springs. To climb it, you must scramble over quite a few boulders and be sure-footed. I consider myself an outdoorswoman, so I'm up for the challenge. It doesn't take long to realize that Larry and his brother, Jon, are both worthy climbers. We climb for what seems like hours, but our climb has only lasted sixty minutes before we stop at the pool above the first falls to cool off and eat sack lunches.

"Well, you are quite the climber," Jon says. "Where'd you learn to climb like that?" he asks.

I know I'm blushing but try to act confident. "I don't know. I guess I was always into outdoorsy stuff."

"I like her," he says, smiling at me. "And I think she just might be a better climber than you, Larry."

"Don't be ridiculous," Larry says, winking at me.

"Well, any gal that can climb like you is more than welcome to join us on other adventures."

I feel so excited. I know that they had approved of me earlier, but a part of me had felt like they were just being nice. But now? This feels more real.

There is something about navigating the outdoors; it brings out everyone's sincere side. Maybe it has something to do with being connected to nature. I don't know, but it always makes me feel at ease to be outdoors.

3

THE BIG QUESTION

"Have a safe trip back to San Diego, hon!" Larry's mom says, giving me a tight hug. "Hope to see you again." Larry's siblings do the same. After all the goodbyes, we climb into his clunky old pickup truck. As he drives us home, I start to sniff the air.

"What are you smelling?" Larry asks.

"Gas," I say, squinching my nose.

"I didn't gas!"

I chuckle. "Not that kind."

He sniffs. "I don't smell a thing."

"Well, I do." I roll my window down.

He shrugs, then rolls his down too. *Guess he can't admit that his precious pickup smells because the gas tank is actually in the cab behind the seat. Oh for goodness' sake.*

It gets uncomfortably quiet in the cab, and I have time to think:

I'm two weeks out from my scheduled departure from San Diego, and it's back to the Pacific Northwest. I've already put out some feelers for auditions in the Seattle area. Hmm …

The silence between us makes it seem as though there's an elephant in the truck. Someone has to break that silence.

I finally say, "Only two weeks left before I leave San Diego. So, what do you think?"

"About what?" he asks, looking at me briefly before returning his focus to the road.

"Marriage," I say, as if we've been talking about it just a few minutes ago. "I kinda need to know what your thoughts are, since I'm either going to stay here or move up to the northwest real soon. I mean …" I hesitate, feeling awkward about it. "Well, the thing is, you probably remember that I said I wouldn't change my plans for anybody except the man I'm going to marry."

"I think we should do it," he says.

I can't believe it. Is he actually saying yes to marriage? I have to be sure.

"Do what?" Now I'm wondering if he might be talking about fixing his pickup, which is going to be my second proposition.

"Get married," he says with a lilt in his voice.

So, here it is. After all the fairy tales and romantic stories that have ever been written and consumed by me, this is his proposal. Well, all that doesn't matter, because the fact is I won't be leaving for Seattle, won't likely be auditioning for the Seattle Symphony, but will be getting married, and I'm so in love. Even though the tone of the proposal could have easily been mistaken as a negotiation for buying his truck, I know he loves me. He just hasn't been well versed in the down-on-one-knee maneuver.

LOVE IS PUT TO THE TEST

An opportunity presents itself, a kind of litmus test of Larry's love. A few days after the "get married" talk, I graduated to serving at a steak and lobster house on the beach in

Del Mar. It is only a four-hour shift and I'm not on a regular schedule. As a college graduate, I do get called to fill in now and then. At the Vagabond, I'd gotten $5 tips from the guys who were only getting coffee and doughnuts. At the steak and lobster house, tips range from $50 to $100. I just treat the customers like princes and princesses—they respond in kind with a good tip.

The phone rings an hour before my shift tonight. "Hi, Janna, my love."

"Hey, babe," I chirp, with a contrived tone of confidence.

"My mom just called to remind me of the Commandant's Ball at Army-Navy Academy in Carlsbad tomorrow night, where I graduated. My brother Jon is set to graduate soon, so it's a big deal."

"Oh yeah. Your mom finagled you a scholarship there since you were such an unruly kid, right?"

"OK, don't rub my face in it now."

"Just kidding."

"Good, because I want you to come. You will, won't you? It would mean a lot to me since it's my brother's senior year."

"Shoot. I can't. Remember, I agreed to work the night shift at the steak house."

"Can't you get out of that?"

My wheels start turning. "Well, I'd like to. But I don't want to burn my bridges. We will be so very tight on money, remember? If I let them down, they probably won't call me again. That's how it works when you're a sub."

"Darn. I so want you to come. My mom and sister Dani are coming too."

"So sorry, babe. I really am. I'll just have to come to the next one."

"OK," he says disappointedly. "So, I'll see you later today after my classes, right?"

"You bet. Love you."

"Love you too."

The next day we are sharing lunch outside the music department. After a peck on the cheek and a hug, he leaves to get his suit ironed per Army-Navy Academy standards. I'm off to do a couple of flute lessons and then to get ready for my evening waitress shift. *This is truly a unique win-win proposition for me.*

My beautiful, full-length bright pink gown from my senior flute recital is still in the closet. After donning my black-and-white server getup, I grab the gown and pop into the cute little white Volvo I'd purchased a month or so ago and head for the steak house.

Just as I was hoping, the manager agrees that I can go ahead and leave early at 7 p.m. I head to the Army and Navy Academy in nearby Carlsbad, where Larry and the family are attending the formal winter event. There will be cookies, punch, and a live band. And the girls from the nearby all-girls private Catholic school will be bused in to dance with the cadets.

Will Larry have his arm draped over one of them? Or will he maybe be just a little too friendly with their older sisters? While I don't think this will be the scenario, it is, in fact, a brilliant plan that I show up unannounced ... an audition of sorts. An audition of his trustworthiness.

After finding a parking spot a few blocks away, I head to the school on foot. As I approach the campus, I see the gym and my heart races a bit.

What should I do if he's with a girl? Turn around and leave or boldly step up?

There he is, alone—eating a cookie, watching his mom and Jon dance together. After watching him for a few minutes, I breathe a sigh of relief. As my confidence rises, I square my shoulders, lift my chin, and walk boldly across the dance floor to my beloved. When he turns his head and sees me approaching, his face lights up and we fall into each other's arms.

"You're here," he exclaims. "I can't believe it."

He has definitely passed the test.

As we laugh, dance, and eat cookies with the family, I nuzzle up to him. "Yes, I will … I will marry you," I whisper in his ear. With no thought of discretion, we kiss, at first lightly, then passionately. When finally I realize there are other people around us, I loosen my hold a bit, looking up into his eyes. He smiles and nods his head to the left. Dani is watching.

"Do you two have something you want to tell us?" she asks.

We glance at each other and nod. "We're going to get married," Larry proclaims.

Having the best time ever, I start to feel more and more a part of this Wagner family. Now I'm fully committed. I have wrestled down the demons of distrust and beg them to leave me alone.

It turns out we can both be serious about the things that truly matter. At the same time, we joke a lot. I love that. It's one of the many things I love about Larry. He'll make a good husband and father not only because of what he'd told me about his father, how little time he got with him and how he wanted to do better himself, but also because he has a tender heart—maybe because the one thing he could count on as he grew up was his mom. Dads came and went, but Mom could always be counted on to stay the course. He has a healthy respect for women, and that suits me just fine. *I am trusting that this is you, God, answering my prayer.*

◆　◆　◆　◆

As the wedding draws near, money is getting tighter. We're both aware that there is no money set aside for a wedding or payment of school tuition bills. We will be watching out for each other. Larry still has three or four months' worth of living expenses set aside from his prior summer job. For my part, I've taken on an au pair job for a family in nearby Mission Hills. And I land a part-time job at the Chinese Community Church in Southeast San Diego.

We decide on an outdoor wedding at the Café del Rey Moro in Balboa Park, San Diego. During a meeting with the wedding manager, she asks about our employment.

"We're musicians," Larry says.

"Oh?" Her eyes widen. "Do you ever do music for weddings?"

"Oh, yes!"

"I'll keep that in mind. Almost every bride asks for a music recommendation," she says. "After your honeymoon, let's get together for an audition here in my office."

As we walk out, I turn to Larry. "Did you happen to notice how many weddings she had on her calendar for the next month?"

"No, were there a lot?"

"I counted seven for just the first weekend alone."

Walking to the car, we are giddy about the possibility of providing live music to some of the hundreds of weddings that occur at this popular spot each summer.

"We're not even married yet," I say, "and the opportunity to make up for your decision not to work in Alaska this summer presents itself."

"Apparently."

OUR WEDDING DAY

Outside of our families, most of the people who are at the wedding today are fellow musicians, martial art friends, and members of the Chinese Community Church. In all, it is an eclectic group of people. My four flutist friends who agreed to perform at the wedding are here, playing my arrangement of two of Larry's original compositions that call for two flutes, a bass flute, and piccolo, soon to be played as each of us walk down the aisle of this outdoor Prado.

My dad is to give me away.

As Dad and I walk down the carpeted aisle, arms linked, so many emotions well up inside as all eyes of the guests and surrounding park-goers are riveted on us, sharing in the joy of the event.

Dad looks sharp in his classic black tuxedo. And I feel somewhat like a princess in my creamy-white satin wedding dress with its six-foot train, the same dress my mom wore some 36 years ago when she walked down the aisle to meet my dad at the pulpit on their wedding day.

As we reach the last terrace above the bubbling fountain, all I see is Larry. Dad and I stop, as planned, so Larry can sing the original song he'd written for me, a song never heard by anyone until this moment:

I've been waiting for you, knocking at love's door.
Did you ever think that you'd have me evermore?
I've only known how to live alone, but now that you've captured me,
Walkin' on down this long hard road, together we can be free.
So many want to know, "How long will love grow?"
I simply smile and let them know, forever and ever.
All the changing seasons that come and pass us by—
Will never take our love away, will never make it dry.
I've only known how to live alone, but now that you've captured me,
Walkin' on down this long hard road, together we can be free.

By the time he finishes, everyone has run out of tissues. He promises to sing this song to me each year on our anniversary.

4

LET'S MAKE A FAMILY

I enjoy caffeine, but during this pregnancy, I have to be careful not to consume too much of it.

"You'll need to limit your caffeine intake to less than 200 milligrams per day, about one 11-ounce cup of coffee," Dr. Lapp warns me on this, my third try for a successful pregnancy.

I'm so tired. Maybe some herbal tea will pep me up. No, maybe it has caffeine … So, maybe hot water? As I toss around that idea in my head, *it* starts. After thirty minutes I know it's my menstrual cycle, acting up the same way it had when I miscarried. I'm panicked. *I can't suffer another miscarriage. I just don't think I can bear the sorrow again. I'll call my friend Sarah. She's an expert on homeopathic cures. Maybe she'll have some ideas.*

"Sarah," I cry out, "I'm having cramps just like the ones I had when I miscarried. Please help me—I'm desperate!"

"Are the cramps strong?" she asks calmly.

"Yes, and there are blood spots."

"Well, I've got your back. I'll be your coach. Lie on your back, with your legs elevated," she says. "Keep breathing calmly and shallowly. I will be there in five minutes."

Click! goes her phone.

◆ ◆ ◆ ◆

Back when I was pregnant the second time, we had moved to a nicer (and slightly larger) rental in La Mesa that had room for a nursery. Well-meaning friends had gently suggested that I might want to wait on the nursery decorating until I passed that critical three-month mark. But something about the cottage's spaciousness and cleanliness (and my impatience) made me feel like the odds were in my favor.

I went to Joanne's Fabric to choose the colors for the quilt I would make, matching the colors with the crib skirt and pillowcases I'd already completed. *OK, OK,* I say to myself. *I will take a couple of days of rest now.*

Maybe I should have shown more restraint. Maybe the loss of that second baby had been like the fourth domino, and a fifth domino is following.

In this third pregnancy, though, that critical three-month milestone had come and gone, so it appeared I was in the clear, and I was relieved that nothing had gone wrong. I lifted my head to heaven, saying a quick thank you.

Now, three days later, the cramps and spotting begin, and the heartbreak rips at my gut.

My hope is fading. "Help me, God," I call out.

Pastor Gregg emphasizes memorizing scriptures, not just for times of crisis, but to help each of us stay on the right path amidst life's challenges. As I take another calming breath, one of those scriptures drops into my mind … perfect for the moment. "No good thing will he withhold from them that walk uprightly." I check myself to see if I've been on the right path of late and if there's anything I need to apologize about. Then I close my eyes, quietly saying the scripture again and again, trying hard to believe that it will be true for me today.

When Sarah arrives, she holds me as I break down and begin to weep.

"Oh, Sarah, do you think this might just be a little spotting? Do you think that there's hope?"

"Yes, Janna, there's always hope. Don't give up. You're past that critical three-month milestone, remember? Maybe this is just some passing spotting, and things will all look bright tomorrow."

"OK, I'll try."

She has a thermos full of what she says is raspberry tea. "Keep breathing calmly and drink as much of this stuff as you can. My mom taught me that it works for muscle cramps, so why wouldn't it work for this?"

The cramping stops, the spotting ends, and I am not miscarrying on this day.

THIS CAN'T BE

The nurse walks me into my room and gives me a gown to put on. As she checks my vitals, she seems a bit anxious, hurried. Five minutes later, she and Dr. Lapp enter the room.

"I am going to go ahead and do an ultrasound," he says.

"OK." I'm excited. I had hoped for this. The gel he applies to my tummy chills my skin and is a bit uncomfortable. It doesn't help that the looks he and the nurse have on their faces are difficult to read, stoic. Dr. Lapp explains that ultrasounds are not very clear and show little detail.

"It's like looking at vague shadows," he tells me. "Almost like looking for what isn't there rather than what is there. And the heartbeats aren't nearly as distinct as you might hope."

My emotions are off the chart. Settle down!

After a few minutes, Dr. Lapp says, "There's a heartbeat!" I smile with such relief and begin to tear up.

Before I can reflect for long, I notice he looks puzzled again!

"What is it?" I ask. "You can be honest." I pretend to be strong.

He says, "Here's another heartbeat."

What? Twins?! "Yes!" I shout.

He keeps moving the device around on my tummy. After a little pause, he moves it again, then stops.

"What's that look?" I ask.

"Here's a third heartbeat!" he exclaims.

"Can I see them on the monitor?" I ask.

"Oh, well—it's difficult to see clearly with all the shadows," he continues. "I can't even tell you the gender, as they are constantly in motion during this ultrasound. But I most definitely was able to hear three heartbeats. You are pregnant with triplets!"

I am absolutely thrilled and want to tell Larry immediately, but he's teaching classes at the music school. It is a bit ironic, because earlier we had discussed that maybe we should have just one child and call it quits. Well, I guess God has something else in mind!

After the doctor leaves the room, and as the nurse is cleaning me up, I ask, "How did the doctor know to give me an ultrasound early on?"

"Well, you are rather large 'for date,' and already wearing a loose maternity shirt. That was the clue."

I barely notice my feet hitting the ground as I go through the waiting room on the way out. *How should I reveal the good news to Larry?*

I want to shout, "I'm having triplets!" to the people in the waiting room as I float by.

I'd better not. Who knows what kind of news they are in for? I don't want to chance sharing my good news, lest I worsen someone else's day.

On the way to my car, I pass a coffee shop/deli that has some really cute disposable placemats at the counter.

It's worth a shot.

"Come on in. You can sit anywhere," the girl behind the counter says.

"Thanks."

"What can I get you?"

"Well, actually, I have an odd request."

"What's that?"

"Well, you see, I just found out that I'm going to have triplets." That's where I lose her.

"Excuse me, what did you just say?"

"My obstetrician just told me I'm carrying triplets."

"Oh, my! Do you want to sit at one of the booths? Would that make you more comfortable?"

"Oh no, I'm fine! I'm just trying to figure out how to tell my husband."

"Are you serious? He doesn't know yet?"

"No, I just found out myself."

"You mean today?!"

"Yes, about fifteen minutes ago. And I was just on the way to my car when I saw your shop."

"Are you going to be OK? Do you need someone to walk you to your car?"

She's so cute, so sweet, and kind. I give a little chuckle. "Nah, I'm fine. I'm thinking of going back to the music school office to work for a couple of hours until my husband gets off work."

"Are you kidding? You are NOT going to work. No way. Go tell your husband and let the rest of the world take care of itself today. This is a BIG deal."

I look down at my big belly and chuckle again. "Oh no, that's not the big deal I was referring to," she says awkwardly. "What I meant … I just mean you should make the day memorable. Go out for dinner or have him give you a foot massage." With that, I begin to tell her my idea.

Make Room—We're Not Alone

Everyone in the deli knows my story by now, so I share my idea with all of them.

"If I can use a placemat to make a card for my husband, I can surprise him with a little notice at our music school, where he's working today. It's just down the hill in the Morena area, near the big nursery and Toys 'R' Us."

So, all of us are writing on the card together. Anyone who walks into the deli is encouraged to be a part of it.

There are so many thoughts going through my head as I approach the studio. Larry is presenting a fun-filled piano lesson to a class of eight-year-olds. As usual, the parents are in attendance, each happily supporting their child's interest in music. They are all having a great time in a circle, playing music flash card games on the carpet.

Normally, I would walk in quietly and slowly, trying not to distract the kids. But not this time! I march right to the center of the children's circle, shoving my ready-made card into Larry's hands. He gives me a look as if to say, "Why are you interrupting me?"

"Read the card!" I say.

The card reads: *"You are going to be the proud father of triplets!"*

This time he looks at me with his mouth open. *"What?!"*

"Read it to the class," I say.

He reads it aloud. *I still don't think he understands what it's saying.*

"It's not a prank," I say.

Just sitting there, along with the parents (who are looking over at me intermittently), he stares at me. I give him a big hug.

He asks, "Is this true?"

The parents and kids are all excited about the news, as they let out some whoops and hollers.

We step outside for a brief moment to hug and kiss.

But, ever the faithful teacher, he tells me, "I'll finish teaching this last class before we get crazy together about this, OK?"

So responsible. I wish I had a camera with me to capture this moment. I guess I'll just have to settle on my memory.

5

MOTHER'S DAY PARADE

It's Mother's Day, and I am in my sixth month of pregnancy. "I want to go to church for Mother's Day, honey. What do you think?"

"I think you are very brave."

"Funny, how perceptions change over the years."

"What do you mean?" he asks.

"Remember that I told you my mom had been unyielding about me buying my clothes with my allowance money, wanting me to sew them myself, starting at age 11 or so? Well, here I am now, 17 years later, grown out of all my maternity clothes, and what am I doing? I'm making things that look like something other than a big gunnysack! Could you take a picture of me, honey? I want to send it to Mom with a thank-you note. She'll be glad I shared my new maternity style this Mother's Day weekend."

We've been attending the Young Married class at *Faith Chapel* for a while but opted to spend Sundays at home once my girth reached 51 inches and I could no longer walk more than a few steps in a row.

"Are you sure you should be doing this, honey?" Larry asks.

"No, but I'm sure I'm going to give it a go."

Arriving late, we see it's already packed. A lovely young lady with chestnut hair and her tall, slim, light-haired husband is waving at us. *She must notice our predicament.*

"Look, Larry, that lady is waving us up to their seats in the front row. She must be a mother herself because she is wearing a corsage."

The lady and her husband have no hesitation when they see a woman, possibly about to give birth, in need of a chair.

Larry takes my arm, and an usher holds my other elbow as we head right down to the very front row of the church.

The service is uplifting. It helps me put to rest the concerns I have about this high-risk pregnancy of mine.

One of the greeters must have overheard me say something in the lobby to another church member about having triplets, because here is the pastor congratulating me and Larry, in front of the entire church body. We came to this church just a few months ago as strangers, but they are treating us like part of the family and are vowing to check in on my well-being frequently through the upcoming months.

MAKING EVEN MORE ROOM

I've taken up the nasty habit of ingesting two tablespoons of cottage cheese every thirty minutes, to make sure that the fetuses entrusted to me get their protein. Here I am, not at all hungry, but the timer is ringing. Somehow, I have to squeeze in that cottage cheese. Sitting on the sofa, I lean to the right and back. One little person is riding up so high that I can't get food down my throat without moving him or her down a little somehow.

"Hello, my precious baby, it's that time again. I don't know who you are yet, but I sure do know where you like to hang out these days. We need to make some room so you and your siblings can get some nutrition. Here we go … work with me now." I take a deep breath, massaging my little person's head down and out from the bottom of my rib cage, right by my solar plexus. I have to shove the cottage cheese in my mouth and down my throat real fast before that babe drifts back up to close the gap again.

"There, we got it," I say. "Good teamwork."

The Happy Pregnancy Blues

Larry and I have been married a little over five years by the time I finally get pregnant with these triplets. Things he and I have taken for granted have now become a cause for concern. We've covered the electrical outlets, but we know it won't be enough. Any of the house décors that are lower than four feet are now moved up, well out of the curious grips of babies. Our house now looks more like … well, something other than an adult dwelling space, but at least it's babyproof.

People with money probably have the convenience of not having to think too much about it. They can maybe hire some help, or figure things out as they go.

We do not have that convenience. We need to have every-thing in order well before the babies arrive. I guess that still does not excuse us from failing to consider how we can cover baby delivery costs. When we thought we were only going to have one child, we figured the bill wouldn't be that bad—manageable at the very least, because we'd planned to stay in the hospital for only a night. But now that we know we are having three babies, financial adjustments will have to be made.

Insurance is mandatory. So, insurance shopping is a challenge. It's difficult being young and broke and having a preexisting condition. Insurers are leery. The insurance industry is not known for gambling. They like a safe bet. Fortunately, we manage to stumble upon an HMO startup company that is willing to cover us, preexisting conditions and all.

"Hi, love," Larry says, walking in the door, setting down his briefcase. "Tired?"

"Hey, babe, glad you're home. I am just lying here reflecting, but yes, I am tired. There's some spaghetti on the stove that you can heat up. Do you mind nuking the vegetables? I feel just a little bit too tired to waddle over there."

"You about ready for bed?" he asks.

"Yep, I'm calling it a day. We have that music gig together at Café del Rey Moro tomorrow. Think I'd better get some sleep. What do you say?"

"Yeah, about the gigs. I'm thinking this should be your last gig until after our three babies are born."

"What? Do you think I look chubby or something?" I say with a laugh.

"You always look beautiful to me, Janna, but I'm just thinking it's not fair to you, and maybe it looks a little bit weird to the people at the wedding."

"I think you have a point there. So, no more gigs on the calendar for me, right? You're going solo."

"I don't think we have a choice. I've got all my tracks programmed in my synthesizer. I'll play the piano part live and the synth will accompany me, so it will be a step up from just a recording … minus the flute and the beautiful blonde standing beside me, of course."

"Aww, aren't you sweet? I don't think anybody's looked at me as a beautiful blonde for quite some time now."

"Well then, they're blind. You're always beautiful in my eyes."

Our Last Gig—Finds Me Big

It's a sweltering summer day, so hot that I feel like my eyelashes are sweating. Larry pulls up to the loading zone, near the outdoor fountain. He flips on the flashers so he can unload. Our Datsun pickup truck is filled to the gills with music equipment.

After unloading me and the equipment near the back entrance, Larry says, "OK, Janna, you can lean against this wall and I'll be back in a flash."

"Exactly what I had in mind."

Larry parks, getting back in no time. He pushes the loaded utility cart as I grab my flute and shoulder bag. We walk over to the gig site, on the first of the three terraces, our usual setup spot. As I put the head, body, and foot of my flute together, I feel like I am being watched. An awkward tension climbs up my spine as I begin my usual warm-up—long tones, scales, and arpeggios, as I wait for Larry to get his gear in place.

I am relieved to see him walk back toward me. I feel some of the eyes shift to him, away from looking at me in my hugeness, being 5 feet 6 and 190 pounds by now.

The guests begin to arrive, and I notice that there is one lady in particular who can hardly keep from staring at me. I'm fairly sure she's the mother of the bride. *I know that Larry will go over to confirm all the details with her in just a moment. Hopefully, that will set her at ease.* She is clearly anxious and discreetly makes her way around behind me and up to Larry, turning her back toward me. She looks concerned and doubtful, perhaps wondering if I'll be OK. *I'm quite sure she has visions of my water breaking right in the middle of the ceremony!*

As we pack up our gear at the end of the wedding, I turn to Larry. "You're right, it's time for me to stop doing the gigs!"

GET TO BED

"I am prescribing bed rest," Dr. Lapp says matter-of-factly over the phone. "And I am prescribing medicine to suppress your contractions."

"I can embrace the medicine part, Doctor," I respond. "But I'm not all too excited about bed rest. I like to exercise, and I like to get things done."

"I don't recommend you get out of bed except to go to the bathroom."

In a spirit of humoring him, I say, "You are so right, thanks for that."

So, here I am today, ignoring his recommendation, figuring I'll start that "bed rest regimen" in a few days. I risk walking short distances. Still, it is clear that I need to limit my walking to an absolute minimum. I can't waddle fifteen feet without feeling like I'm going into labor.

Eventually, Larry procures a wheelchair so he can roll me around. I'm in that wheelchair everywhere. I chuckle when people stare at us as we cruise through the grocery store aisles, or on the La Jolla boardwalk. He pushes and pushes until he builds up enough speed to hop on the back as we glide along the boardwalk's cliffside path or the grocery aisle at Gemco. He always knows when it's okay to be childish, seeking adventure. I, on the other hand, am terrified. I wonder what other people think when they see me and Larry in such a playful, blissful state. Maybe it makes them smile, or maybe they think we're insane.

Getting Closer to D-day

It's a sweltering summer day—80 degrees in the shade. We have no air conditioning. I'm the antithesis of blissful. I'm eight months pregnant, and our next-door neighbors have invited us to a pool party. Larry's there now, but I'm staying home. It's a party, but it's a struggle for me to get out of the bed or off the couch. Forget about trying to sit on one of those folding pool chairs; I'd bust right through it.

Larry gets back after about twenty minutes.

"Come on, honey," he says, attempting to cajole me into joining the fun.

"It's so nice outside. Everyone's having a blast—you would too, babe, if you'd just give it a go. I promise I'll bring you right home if you feel uneasy."

I make a pouty face and fold my arms.

"All your friends are dying to see you." He keeps nagging me for a few more minutes.

"Fine, I'll come."

Our neighbors, Ted and Shirley, have set up a little poolside area for me, which is simply a lounge chair, and a little wading pool for me to cool my feet in. But that's all I need.

Lying here, I can't help but think that if this were a month ago, I would have been in the pool, enjoying the bliss of weightlessness, not feeling like a fatty. Now, the pool just taunts me, reminding me of how much bigger I've become, with every joint swelled up to near full capacity from water retention.

Suddenly, without warning, my chair snaps in half just like a toothpick!

They see me on the ground and breaths are drawn in. I'm in shock, but still feeling a bit silly, so I laugh to hide my embarrassment. Laughter may be good medicine, but when everyone sees me laughing, they all join in, and that medicine doesn't taste so good. There is an awkward pause. I burst into tears, feeling as if they are laughing at me instead of with me. Damn these pregnancy hormones. Because I'm unable to control my tears, Larry puts his arm around me to take me home.

"Hey, guys, I'm just going to take the little lady home and dust her off," he says.

It is probably a lot more awkward for them than for me, but I'm way beyond trying to smooth things over. I just want the water to break so we can get on to the fun part, meeting our three babies face to face.

6

ALMOST TIME NOW!

We are forever trying different ways to make me comfortable. Currently, sitting in a cool bath, pouring lukewarm water over my shoulders brings the most relief. I finally cave in to the doctor's request for full rest. I'm fairly helpless and can't even keep up the bookkeeping for the music school.

At peace with the decision to let go, I sleep better for the next couple of days. Until I remember that Larry still has a gig coming up and it's out of town.

"Make sure you come ASAP if I call you about my water breaking," I tell him. "Don't even hesitate for an instant, OK? I'm almost full term now."

"I will," he says, smirking. "Do you think I'd miss something as miraculous as the birth of our children?"

My due date is not here yet, but I feel very uneasy about him driving up to LA, leaving me here in San Diego.

"You promise?"

"Promise."

"How much do I have to fuss to get you not to take the gig?"

He tips his head with a reassuring smile but is silent.

"Never mind," I say, "I know we need the money."

So, while Larry is off earning a paycheck, a hundred miles away in LA, I am left in the care of some kind neighbors, who are also dear friends, Claudia and her two daughters, Lisa and Tanya.

While Larry is at his music gig, Claudia suggests we make a day of it.

"Let's all go to La Jolla Shores," she says. "You, me, and the girls. After all, it *is* the 4th of July."

The sun is out, and the sky is as blue as a spectacular San Diego blue sky. The beach is packed with all sorts of people … some lounging, others tossing a Frisbee, and there are even some amateur sand artists constructing complex sandcastles.

"Wow, what a day!" Lisa says, as if this were not a standard day in San Diego. Claudia and the girls are all wearing 4th of July-themed swimwear. Not me. I am the *Torpedo Lady*. That's what Larry calls me now, because to him my tummy looks like a torpedo had hit me from behind but didn't go all the way through. It's not as harsh as it sounds. Besides, I agree, it's true. I'm wearing a black bikini bottom with a huge navy-blue maternity top that's filled with wild triangle patterns. And huge as it is, it doesn't quite cover the bottom of my belly.

Boy, do I get the stares. The sideways looks people give me are the worst. I even see a couple of people sneak a photo of *Torpedo Lady*.

"Everyone is staring," I say.

"Because you're so beautiful," Tanya says.

"It's true," Claudia says. *She must be responding to the look of doubt on my face.*

I want to believe them, but my insecurity keeps getting the best of me, sopping up all my confidence. I hate being like this—this isn't my normal self. Usually, I'd be having fun.

Eventually, the girls convince me to at least dip my toes in the water. "Ah, this is sheer bliss!" I thrust my arms out to the sides and gaze at the sky; I almost feel like I can stand on my tippy toes, reach up, and touch it. At this moment, as the water sloshes around my ankles and the sun shines on me, I truly feel as if I am in God's presence. At this moment, nothing else matters. My insecurity dissolves into peace.

On the drive home, there is traffic—a lot of it. I can tell Claudia is concerned because she keeps nibbling at her bottom lip the way she always does when she's nervous about something, which is seldom. *She is probably concerned that I might go into labor at any moment.* Strangely, her worrying comforts me; it's nice to know I have such a caring friend.

Larry gets back from his gig at the same time I get back from the beach. What timing. *God is good.*

A WATER BREAK?

It has been nearly impossible lately to get comfortable in bed with all that baby weight and fluids pushing down on me. Often, I end up climbing out quietly and waddling to the bathroom to start a warm bath.

"Ahhh." This warm water is wonderful … relaxing. So relaxing that I doze off.

By now, though, it is almost time for the sun to rise. I carefully slide my huge self out of the tub, dry off, and throw my towel to the side. Just as I begin to shuffle back to the bedroom, it happens.

"Larry, my water broke!"

Larry lifts his head off the pillow and asks sleepily, "Are you sure?"

I wonder how many other women have heard those same words.

"Yes!" I shout.

At this response, Larry shoots up. He is curbing his enthusiasm by doing a fact check.

"Wait. You just got out of the bath, right?"

Unbelievable. I stare at him in disbelief. Am I going to have to verify this observation?

"Is there a chance you maybe didn't dry off completely?"

I point to the puddle on the floor and bite my tongue.

"Right!" he exclaims.

He jumps up like a fireman responding to an alarm … only without any order. First putting on his jeans. Then running around trying to remember what he is supposed to bring to the hospital. I point to the Lamaze bag.

"Right!" Grabbing it, he lovingly wraps my robe around me. Then he pauses, runs back to the bedroom, and returns with a camera in his hands. He looks at me and smiles apologetically as he slips the towel off my shoulders and takes a snapshot, saying, "I want to remember this day always."

He wraps the towel back around my waist. A quick call to the doctor to alert him of our departure, and we are out the door. We lock the door and I stand for a moment on the top stair of our steep walkway to catch my breath. It's 5 a.m.

Gathering a respectable flutist's lungful of air, I shout out to the universe, "MY WATER BROKE! WE'RE GOING TO THE HOSPITAL TO HAVE OUR BABIES!" Someone calls back, "I'LL TELL THE REST OF THE NEIGHBORHOOD" … and I waddle down the steps, with Larry's help. I feel like I have truly arrived!

In the car, I can tell Larry is nervous because his left knee won't stop jittering. With one hand on the steering wheel, the other entwined with mine, the drive proceeds in suppressed chaos. Both of us are doing all we can to stay calm despite my moans as the contractions are getting stronger. Though I'm not all smiles at the moment, I am still grateful to have Larry right there beside me, my husband, soon to be the father of our children.

This moment reminds me how awesome God is, and how he has always blessed me, but not without first presenting me with my fair share of challenges, like when Larry and I first met. That bout with pleurisy had forced me to postpone my recital by six months. As I recovered, I started to visit the practice rooms again, getting ready for round two, my second effort at a senior solo recital. Without that bout with pleurisy would I have run into Larry that day in the practice rooms? Would he be my husband, and the soon-to-be father of our triplets?

SURPRISES AT THE HOSPITAL

Once we are in the door, Larry takes on the full persona of a lead performer. You'd think I had no part in the event. He is in "gig" mode, making sure everyone is being entertained.

Dr. Lapp arrives at about 6 a.m. He examines me and evaluates the options, which includes another ultrasound. I listen carefully to his conclusions, thrilled that he has heard strong heartbeats.

"Janna, it looks like one of the fetuses is traverse, a position that is not unexpected in cases of multiples."

"Traversed?"

"It is lying sideways."

I'm crushed. This means I need a C-section.

"My nurse will be back in a few minutes to explain the prep for your procedure."

I drop my head in defeat and mope. Larry strokes my head and kisses my cheek.

"This will work out, honey. You'll see."

The door closes.

"Here comes a contraction." I moan. Larry is doing his best to get me breathing in perfect Lamaze mode. It is his playful antics that lighten my mood the most. Somehow, he can always get me to chuckle.

THE BIG EVENT

After about three hours of labor, as the obstetric team is assembling for the birth of multiples, I've had enough fun with this Lamaze thing. The anesthesiologist comes in and explains the process ahead of time, calming my nerves and gaining my confidence. At this point, I am quite agreeable about getting a pelvic block. I feel like hollering, "Bring it on, I'm ready! Let's do this!"

This birth will be difficult, both emotionally and physically. I want ever so desperately for the whole thing to be over.

When the team is assembled, I am wheeled into the operating room. While I am being prepped for a well-rehearsed medical procedure, I scan the room and see no less than fifteen people in full scrubs surrounding the glass wall of the room with all eyes on me. It looks like my turn to be on center stage.

The anesthesiologist finishes his part to get me ready, and I'm all strapped down on the table. *Are they afraid I might try to escape?* Larry is ushered in to join the party. He walks in with his head high, nodding a welcome to each member of the entourage.

We make eye contact, and he sobers. I nod to him in desperation, as if to say, "Get over here, please, right now!"

He strokes my head and holds my hand as I bark, "I need you to keep holding my hand and looking me in the eye the WHOLE time. Don't look away from me. I need you!"

It's been only minutes since the team started and they've already delivered the three babies, one minute apart, which includes checking their vitals and genders and wiping them off to show us their faces. They let Larry hold each one for a brief moment.

With the first delivery, the doctor says: "It's a boy." Then I hear a cry, the team wipes the baby down, and glances back at us.

With baby number two, "It's a boy."

Baby three, "It's a boy."

"Oh, wow!" I say. The obstetrician looks up and makes eye contact with the pediatrician, who says, "Wait. I think there is one more. Is there another?"

Larry takes his eyes off me and I cry, "Look at me!"

"Yes, there is," exclaims the pediatrician. He looks at Larry, but Larry has his eyes glued on me.

"This will be your girl," says Dr. Lapp. "There's an apple stem. It's another boy!"

To which I say, "God Help Me!"

Larry grins from ear to ear, and the buzz in the room is electric.

"Janna," Larry says, but can't finish the thought.

When the nurse puts my fourth baby in my arms, it finally dawns on me. *Quadruplets.*

PART TWO

7

IN THE LIMELIGHT

Larry has been a busy little bee with the press. The hospital's public relations department sets up special times for the various news agencies, both TV and print, to do interviews. My job is to rest and walk. Walking is crazy painful at first—torture. But with each session, I go further and feel less pain.

"Hey, darling," Larry says. "Don't get up, but let me read to you, OK? We've been mentioned on Good Morning America and every news station in town. This is from our local paper." He pauses. "Are you okay if I read it to you?"

"Can I have some yogurt and juice first?" I say sleepily.

He's all energetic and perky, having no problem with all this attention … loving it really.

"Here you go, babe. Are you good to go now, Jan?" He pauses.

"Yep, bring it on."

After a minute he begins:

July 9, 1981, by Maureen Doe

It doesn't happen very often—one in 512,000, according to some estimates—but two La Mesans just became the parents of quadruplets.

Larry Wagner stood by as his wife, Janna, gave birth to four boys on Monday between 9:44 a.m. and 9:47 a.m. It's the second time such an event has happened in San Diego County and the first time for all four to be of the same sex. According to H. Bailey Gallison, public relations director at Mercy Hospital where the babies were born, no one can find any statistics on how rare that might be. Larry, 28, said his first reaction was disbelief. Janna, 29, said she was "pretty shocked." But the feeling around the hospital, where Janna will stay until this weekend, was happiness and excitement.

"Everyone just went crazy (when they heard)," said Rebecca Dierker, R. N., Supervisor of the OB/GYN floor. "One of the nurses in the delivery room yelled out the news. We called admissions. Everyone knew within minutes. It boosted morale around here."

The Wagners, who have no other children, also appeared happy although somewhat in shock. Janna's physician, Dr. Dale Lapp, had predicted triplets, so the Wagners were not totally unprepared. A sonogram had been done and the outline of three babies had been seen.

As Janna said, "What's one more? At least they can all share a room for a long time."

The Wagners have a two-bedroom house in La Mesa and space is going to be one of their biggest problems. As for help with the kids, right now they are set. "Janna's mom and dad are coming in from Seattle," said Larry, "and the next-door neighbor, Grammy Jean, will come in four days of the week. And I'll be there."

But money might be another problem. Larry said he is open to the idea of endorsing some baby products. If the boys could generate some financial backing just by their very presence, he said he wouldn't turn it down. "I would welcome it. At a young age they are not aware of what they wear," he said. "As they get older, I would want them to be able to make some of their own choices. But we're not afraid of that at first."

He said he would put the money away for college. The Wagners own and operate three music schools in San Diego County. Both are musicians. Larry teaches, and Janna is the business manager. As to whether she will be able to continue now that she has four children, she said, "that's a good question."

But there's no question that the parents hope at least one of the boys will follow in their footsteps and become a musician. "At the very least they will all start listening to music right away," said Larry.

It hasn't yet been determined if the boys are identical or just fraternal. "Blood test results won't be conclusive until next week," said Gallison. But Janna said the latest word was that the doctors felt the boys might be two sets of identical twins.

Janna was prescribed a low-dose medicine to increase her chances of ovulation by 0.1 percent before giving birth. But, said Gallison, doctors don't think that caused the multiple births. Both Janna and Larry have twins in their families.

At this writing, the boys had not been named, although sisters at Mercy Hospital were pushing for Matthew, Mark, Luke, and John. Larry said he and Janna were still discussing names.

The boys are healthy babies and the largest two already are in the regular nursery. The other two are in the intermediate care nursery.

The two biggest boys will probably go home with their mother when she leaves the hospital.

"Babies usually can leave the hospital if they weigh 5 pounds," said Gallison. It's unusual for multiple birth babies to be so healthy, but Janna explained it saying, "We come from good stock."

Her secret for success was good nutrition, taking it easy, and staying off her feet. She said she went into false labor 2½ months ago, which prompted her doctor to prescribe drugs to help her relax. When she shopped, she took precautions such as riding around in a wheelchair.

"And," added Larry, "she drank gallons of milk a day, got lots of protein, and took lots of vitamins."

"The hot weather helped," said Janna, "because it made me so tired, I didn't want to do anything."

All of this contributed to Janna being able to carry the babies to full term, an unusual occurrence in multiple births. One of the Wagners' neighbors has erected a sign in front of the couple's house announcing the population increase. But it won't seem real until the four boys are in their new home.

Janna had two sleeping babies with her at the interview and she asked if it was normal for them to be so quiet. She was assured that it was, and then told, "Just wait until you get them home." The Wagners' house may never be quiet again.

Larry looks up with a quirky smile and his signature chuckle. "We're celebrities, right?"

"You are loving this, I know, but I need you to hold me," I blurt out.

"I could use some of that too," he says.

As we lie on the hospital bed without a word for a while, the phone rings.

Larry answers the phone and as he is handing it to me says, "Jan, it's Mom and Dad."

"How are you doing, Jan?" Mom says.

"Great, Mom. Are you here or in Seattle?"

"We are in town and are hoping to see you in a few minutes. Would that be okay?"

"Absolutely! The babies are waiting to see their grandparents. And Larry's reading one of the news articles to me. They quoted me when I said we come from good stock. Kind of fun to hear that, isn't it? I think you and Dad are going to have a lot of fun with this. Can you believe it, Mom? In one fell swoop, I have four sons to raise. Make that five if you count Larry."

After Mom and Dad arrive, somehow the only thing that matters is what's happening at this very moment. We are full circle, and "family" takes on a whole new meaning for all of us. There are tears and laughter and complete silence as the magnitude of the experience hits us all. Mom and Dad are in their glory, donned in hospital garb and sitting in side-by-side recliners, each holding two of the boys as people take their picture. But no amount of pride can outdo that of Larry—proud father. Now and then I lean over to remind him that I'm actually the one that gave them birth (though he did make his small contribution).

A LITTLE ROMANCE

Just four days after their birth, we're able to share a candlelit dinner. Granted, it is in our double-wide hospital room, but it's still lovely. The staff is even dressed up and playing the parts of restaurant servers, towels over their forearms and all, as they present drinks and entrees.

"Would you like white or red wine?" they ask.

Larry quickly says, "Red, please."

Then turning to me. "Oh, I'm not able to drink wine when I'm breastfeeding," I begin to say with a bit of pride in my voice.

Larry chimes in, "Oh, I'll go ahead and take hers, thanks."

I'm feeling uneasy as I look at him. *This is odd. I've hardly ever seen him drinking, and never more than one serving. Is something going on that I don't know about?*

Larry jumps in with one of his quick-witted quips. "I'll celebrate for the two of us."

They all chuckle and I let it drop for now.

8

HOLLYWOOD BABIES

For the time being, we are all abuzz with the euphoria of being treated like royalty. It's as though we are being protected by a bubble of goodwill. We have no comprehension at all of what the path before us will entail.

I've lost something like sixty pounds in this first week, probably water-weight. Puffiness is gone, my skin is glowing, and my eyes are twinkling with joy. Larry, the consummate entertainer, is still in his element. Celebrity status has its perks.

This bubble feels good. I feel important, cherished, and utterly irreplaceable.

Our pastor, George Gregg, is tipping us off with some encouraging counsel during his visit today.

"God will be there to meet your every need," he says. "Count on it. The thing is, he's seldom early. So, don't lose heart. He may not be early, but he's also never late."

The nurse is in the room, checking my vitals. As Pastor Gregg leaves, she leans into me, and with her hand on my shoulder, says, "If you run into a snag, you will be equipped to face it … sometimes it's better not to know what's on the road ahead of you."

For now, I'm riding a cloud of optimism. I do sense that whatever the future holds, we are embarking on a journey that will test and grow our faith daily.

LOOK AT THAT!

This morning the nurse hands me an envelope with a New York postmark on it. Larry eagerly volunteers to open it.

"Sure, go for it," I reply.

He opens it carefully. He glances at the photo inside and drops his jaw, then busts up laughing, tears of a belly laugh forming in the corners of his eyes.

"What? What is it?" I ask.

Not able to talk through his uncontrollable laughter, he hands it to me.

There I am in living color, *Torpedo Lady*, at the beach, huge and miserable on the 4th of July, my husband nowhere in sight and two days before our babies are born.

I recall that day at the beach, wearing a bikini bottom and a huge tank top. That day as I threw my long blonde hair back out of my face, something caught my eye. It was a man lifting a telephoto lens to his face and looking like he might be pointing it at me. I was miserable and nonplussed, so thought nothing of it.

But now, the circle completes itself. The man was watching the national news when a picture and a story about our family came on the screen. He realized that the lady he had been shooting from afar on July 4 was the very same lady he'd seen at the beach on vacation in San Diego, California—me. He sent the photo to the public relations department at the hospital.

"This one is definitely going on our family photo wall," Larry chides.

"Are you kidding? That is not a picture that a woman, at least this woman, hangs on the wall. But I will agree to keep it for posterity, as I think the coincidence is nothing short of a miracle. It's not very flattering, but it will be a part of our family history." Larry gives me a big bear hug.

I'm being treated with so much regard, like a star at a resort, enduring difficult rehab workouts, but always followed by "Attagirl" and other words of encouragement. I've just finished middle-of-the-night feedings for Chad and Kyle, who are big enough to room with us. Larry is deep asleep in the extra bed, and two nurses whisk away the two babies, get them all cleaned up, and return them to their cribs in our room after each feeding.

I fall back asleep and wake up to see Larry sitting beside me on the bed as the sun begins to emerge from the shadows.

"We are getting so spoiled staying at the hospital," I say. "I could get used to getting cared for this way."

He hugs me. "Hey, baby, I have some news for you," he says.

"Good news?"

"I think you'll like it." He pauses. "Today is going to be wild," he continues. "An entire new stream of reporters is just outside the door, hoping for a photo shoot and celebration."

"Well, they'll have to wait, because it's hair and makeup time."

Larry slips out to hold them off, and I hit the mirror.

When Larry steps back into our double room, he fills me in.

"Oh my gosh, Janna. You're not going to believe it!" he exclaims.

"What now?!"

"Uh, well, the local affiliates of ABC, CBS, NBC, and our local station KUSI are all out there! Not to mention the local papers, the *La Mesa Courier*, the *Daily Californian*, and the *Union-*

Tribune. A few days ago the publicist asked if we'd be okay with them making a big deal of the event, and I said yes. He said the morale around the hospital has been improving since our event, and this could be just the thing to give the hospital staff even more of a boost."

"They have been so good to us," I say. "Bring it on!"

Outside the door, there's a big show as nurses parade out of the hospital nursery one by one to our room, each with a baby in their arms. Then, one by one, they set them in our laps. Though a bit staged, it is nonetheless priceless. It is, without a doubt, showtime. Cameras are everywhere in and out of the room. Now, it's my turn to be in the limelight. But I catch myself. *Okay, let's be real! Larry is the showboat, but at least I get to share the limelight with him.*

As the cameras are rolling, I announce the names we had decided on, in the order of their birth:

Chad Anthony Wagner.

Benjamin Lewis Wagner.

Kyle Elliott Wagner.

Brett Emerson Wagner.

Following that, Bobby Tolan, a hitting coach for the San Diego Padres baseball team, walks in. He is carrying four little baseball caps and four of the smallest Padres kids' outfits I've ever seen. As he walks up gingerly, I wonder if my little guys will ever grow into outfits that are at least four times their size. Next, he presents each of the boys with a baseball, signed by none other than Tony Gwynn and all of the other guys on the team.

It's so fun, and it kind of feels like our life with quads is going to be one big party.

Apparently, it's not enough that Larry watches all the news stations on the TV whenever there is a story about us. Between his flipping the channels around, he pauses.

"Are you okay if I read you this article from the *La Mesa Courier*, Jan?" he asks.

"I suppose, but haven't you seen enough of all the hoopla? After all, we do have all the inside scoop."

He laughs and starts reading:

MORE FROM THE LOCAL NEWSPAPER

Lawrence and Janna Wagner wanted one child and were told they were having triplets. They were stunned when Janna gave birth to four healthy babies, all boys. The quadruplets are the second in San Diego County history and the first born at Mercy Hospital, where more than 185,000 babies have been delivered during the last 91 years."

"Wow," I say. "In 91 years, we are only the second? I guess that does sort of make us ..."

"Famous?" he asks.

"Yeah. But after all this attention, how will we manage when we're out of the limelight?"

"We are in this together. And God is already blessing us. Between the two of us, you being the director and the best mom ever, and me being the loyal helper, we'll get through whatever comes."

He keeps reading:

According to statistics supplied by the hospital's other medical authorities, the odds of quadruplet births are actually more than 800,000 to 1...

As he keeps reading, I doze off.

9

HELP IS ON THE WAY

It's Sunday, July 11, and Pastor Gregg announces to the congregation that we are due to come home with Chad and Kyle any day now. "Let's welcome them with a generous love offering, shall we?" he says.

After the service, one of the ladies suggests, "Let's organize a committee to bring meals to them every day for a while until they get settled in."

The nurse steps into our hospital room quite late, peeking in to see if one of us is awake.

"Come on in," I say. "No need to tiptoe. I need these guys to get used to sleeping through anything. I have a feeling it might get noisy at our place when we get all these guys home."

"A Claudia Sperry called and asked if she might call you. Do you know her?"

"Sure do," I answer. "She's the one that took me to the beach on the 4th of July."

"The 4th of July?" she asks, stunned. "Isn't that just two days before you delivered? And weren't you on bed rest?"

"Uh, yeah," I say hesitantly. "I rested a lot at the beach."

She gives me a doubtful look.

"So, you were saying that Claudia called?" I say quickly.

"Oh, yes. Should I put the call through when she calls back?"

"That would be great."

A little later Claudia rings through. I can't believe the news. As Larry rubs his eyes and begins to wake, I say, "I just spoke with Claudia."

"What'd she say."

"Do you recall that Jean, who lives down the street from us, lost her husband just two months ago?"

"I don't really know her that well, but it was sad to hear."

"Well, Grammy Jean is kind of like famous for helping people when she sees there's a need. And, she thinks we need a bigger car."

"OK."

"Claudia said that the loss of her beloved Scotty after fifty years of marriage has left her with a considerable void. She says it helps heal her sadness when she puts her mind on helping others. Grammy also told her that the car her husband had driven all those years just sits in her garage now, since she never learned to drive. She wants us to have the car."

"That's incredible. I can hardly believe it. I was wondering how we'd get four baby car seats into our Mazda RX-2 sedan. I've never seen it. What's it look like?"

"It's a 1978 Ford sedan. It's like brand-new!"

"We'll have to get good at putting three baby car seats in the backseat and one in the middle of the front seat," Larry says. "But we'll get it down with practice."

"Honey," I say. "I haven't given a single thought as to how we'd manage to transport our unexpected fourth child."

"Well, I have. It'll be cozy, but a big sedan will get the job done just fine."

Back and Forth

At ten days, Chad and Kyle are released to go home. It's both good and bad news. Brett's PKU levels have been corrected and Ben is no longer jaundiced, but the pediatric team wants to keep them at the hospital for observation and so they can gain some weight. As we drive away from the hospital with Chad and Kyle, leaving their two brothers behind, my heart is broken.

As tears stream down my face, Larry tries in vain to comfort me.

"It will just be for a short time, and we'll be going back every day for the feedings," he says.

"I am determined not to leave our babies at home with someone else. I'm so afraid that the boys might get a feeling of me not having enough time or energy for them. I want to take Kyle and Chad with me to the hospital when I go there to feed Ben and Brett."

"Why is that?"

"I want to have my babies with me all the time, every minute, for at least the first month or so."

"How could that work out? I mean, you can't be trying to get two babies out of their car seats, up to the neonatal unit, and then what? You tell them to sit there and be good boys while you feed their brothers?"

"That's where you come in. You and I both will go to the hospital with the bigger guys in tow, and when I'm busy feeding Ben and Brett, you'll have Chad and Kyle with you. You can manage it, I think."

He rolls his eyes and gives me his look that says, "You're making things much more complicated than they need to be."

"While I'm feeding the little guys, you can try out your entertaining antics on the big guys, or you could entertain the hospital staff. You know that's just about your most favorite hobby these days … let's be honest. And hey, someone gave us some very cute front carriers. Maybe you can figure out a way to carry two at once."

FEEDING THE TEAM

In between feedings, while Brett and Ben hang out at neonatal, we sometimes gather the two big boys and transport them to one of our favorite haunts in La Jolla, the boardwalk alongside the cliffs. Today is one of those days. The first order of business after exiting the car is to strap them into the front carriers, one baby on each of our fronts, and we're off.

After a bit of a walk, I say, "Let's rotate the boys now, Larry, so each one gets time to be with each of us."

"Good idea. Man, we are certainly going to need a baby carriage one day. Once we have all four, it's going to be a challenge, right?"

"Maybe, when the time comes, we can have two straps each and put one baby on the front and one on the back—at least until they get heavy. Right now, they feel light as a feather."

We're on the same path that terrorized me when I was seven or eight months pregnant, over 200 pounds, and totally helpless. Larry would jump onto the back of the wheelchair as he pushed me around, gathering speed as he hooted and hollered for my entertainment benefit. Today, though, I have control of my own body, and it's exhilarating to be here and to be walking.

Friday, July 24, 1981, Mercy Hospital Neonatal Department

I'm so tired of getting up early, finding a parking space, and dragging my sorry self up to neonatal. It isn't the feeding of Ben and Brett that I dread. That's a joy. It's the ordeal after each feeding. As soon as my feeding joy is done, I have to turn my babies over to the nursing staff, who put a tube down my guys' throats and suck the breast milk out to measure the volume, to be sure they are getting enough nutrition. My babies fuss and cry until the milk is measured, approved of by one of the nurses, and then returned down their throats to their bellies. Then I hold them and love on them through my tears. The process is called gavage, and I'm told again and again that it is in their best interest.

Today as the boys are at the end of the gavage session, Dr. Lapp walks in.

"Dr. Lapp," I whine, "I am so tired of this routine. When will it ever be over?"

"How about tomorrow?" he asks.

"What? What does that mean?"

"It means Ben and Brett can go home and join their brothers."

"You mean home to stay? You mean we'll all be together?"

"Yep, starting tomorrow morning."

"Oh, thank you, thank you, thank you."

10

DO YOU THINK WE MIGHT GET A FEW WINKS?

It's the kids' naptime, and Larry is down for a nap of his own. As I stand over the boys, I can't take my eyes off them.

Even before I'd given birth to our kids, I knew, or at least assumed, that raising them wouldn't be easy. The assumption was right. The identical boys, Ben and Chad, already show a special affinity for one another, responding to each other's cries and staring at each other. When one cries, so does the other.

For the first six weeks, Brett is only at peace when strapped close to me in a front carrier.

Kyle is usually relaxed, happy to sit back and watch the goings-on of his brothers. Neither of us gets much sleep.

◆　◆　◆　◆

The meals delivered daily by church members are a godsend, as are the four windup baby swings we recently snagged at a thrift store.

Today, after feeding and cuddling the boys, we are putting each one in his swing, head braced with rolled-up towels. The limiting factor is the swing with the shortest swing time: 25 minutes.

"Hey, honey, do you have all of those towels and blankets rolled up to keep their heads steady on the swings?" I ask.

Larry looks up. "Yes, Sergeant Mommy."

"Oh, ha, ha. Okay, let's do this."

He starts on the left, me on the right, winding the swings up, moving toward the center.

We sing softly to them until all are asleep. As soon as the fussing stops, we collapse on the nearby bed to grab a few winks. As the swings start slowing down, we take turns winding them all up again.

Partway through the second windup session, one of them starts to fuss, signaling that it is time to start the routine again—windup, diaper, feed, cuddle, clean up messes, repeat.

For these first three and a half months of their lives, we average little more than 45 minutes of sleep at a time. We've heard of doctors, soldiers, and pilots taking power naps for a boost of energy. That's pretty much the zone we are in.

GRATITUDE AND GUILT

I'm feeling guilty that I can't keep up with thank-you notes to those on the church committee bringing us food every day. I pick up the phone and dial the church office.

"Sharon, I have a confession to make."

"What's that, honey? What can I do to help?"

"I'm so embarrassed." Tears well up and I begin to blubber. "I'm just so overwhelmed. I don't know how to handle this. I feel like such a failure. I should be so grateful, but I feel guilty.

I'm so confused about who brought what, on what day, and in what container."

"Janna, you're doing just fine. We are all so proud of you. Are you feeling like you have to send thank-you notes?"

"Of course. And I can't seem to find the patience to visit with the kind people who are bringing these wonderful meals. How rude is that? And I'll never be able to cook half as well as they do when it's time for me to take over the cooking again."

"Take a deep breath, Janna. It's going to be all right. There you go. Now another. Are you okay now? I have an idea that just might help everyone out. I'll get right back to you in a few minutes."

"Thank you … *sniffle, sniffle.*"

After blowing my nose, I sit down to raise a song of praise to my God, in an effort to change my mood. I sing a familiar praise song. "In his time, in his time—he makes all things beautiful, in his time. Lord, please show me every day, as you're teaching me your way, that you do just what you say—In your time. In your time, in your time—you make all things beautiful, in your time. Lord, my life to you I bring, may each song I have to sing, be to you a lovely thing, in your time."

ENTERTAINING ANGELS UNAWARE

The phone rings again just after I put the boys down for a nap. I hesitate. *I sure hope this isn't gonna make me miss my afternoon nap. Maybe it's Sharon. I'd better answer it.*

"Hi, Janna. Thanks for taking my call," the lady on the other end says.

It's a stranger. "Okay." I hesitate.

"You don't know me, but I've been following your story in the news. Anyway …"

Silence.

"I think you need a bigger house and I'm determined to make that happen for you."

"Wow, really? How can that happen?" I ask skeptically.

"Have you ever heard of Charco Construction?"

"No, I don't think so."

"The owner is my friend, Chuck Swimmer. He says that he's due to collect some favors from his subcontractors and that he wants to work something out for you and your family."

Is this really happening?

"I'll get back to you soon, Janna."

I vacillate between exhilaration and skepticism, finally settling on a "wait and see" attitude.

I feel like a silly little child somehow believing that my Fairy Godmother is going to come along and make everything perfect for me.

No sooner have I hung up than the phone rings again, and Sharon gets back to me.

"You know, Janna, people aren't helping you because they want a thank-you note."

I chuckle and admit, "I guess that's true."

"How about this—I will ask that meals be delivered in disposable containers and without the name of the donor, thereby anonymous. Meals will be set on the counter quietly at the same time each day. Recipes will be included. Will that work for you?"

"Is that OK? Won't people feel that I'm being ungrateful?"

"Don't you worry. I'll make sure they understand the big picture."
She pauses.

"One more thing, Janna. I strongly suggest that you keep a list of each and every thing you can think of that might make life easier for you. Then, when people ask what they can do to help, look at your list and give them a choice or two. Remember, you'll just be following my directions, so don't be tempted to feel guilty. You have to believe that people really do want to help."

◆　◆　◆　◆

Larry comes home from a late night at the music school. When I tell him about today's phone calls, he shakes his head in disbelief and smiles.

"Can you believe it?" I ask. "It's such an expression of love to us."

"Well, my darling, maybe you're morphing into a person who can accept that she needs help. I think you might be a little more vulnerable than you're willing to admit to yourself."

"Will you help me with that?"

"Are you giving me permission to tell you what to do?"

"I wouldn't go that far."

He hugs me and we both chuckle.

BLESSING UPON BLESSING

My mom thinks that I should have a dryer for the laundry. I stubbornly hold my ground and insist that all the laundry be hung outside to dry naturally. Now that my parents have left for home and I'm hanging the laundry on my own, I sure wish I had a dryer. *Newsflash to self, she's right.* Someone at the church catches word of our need for a dryer and the pastor sponsors the purchase of one, which we readily accept.

◆　◆　◆　◆

With Larry still at work, I hear a knock on the door.

"Hi, Janna. I'm Sam—from the church."

"Sam, glad to meet you."

"I looked for you and Larry at church but missed you." He takes an envelope out of his back pocket, stretching his hand out toward me.

"What is this?" I ask.

"I just finished balancing my finances for the month. I seem to have $500.00 more than I need. I'd like for you and Larry to have it."

"Sam, this is the exact amount we are short on our mortgage this month. We just prayed last night to be able to make the payment on time."

"I'm glad to be a part of it," he says.

"So many people ask us how we manage with four all the same age. This is how we do it, Sam—by the grace of God and the extravagant kindness of friends, some of whom we've never met before. Thank you, Sam."

As I think about this and the many blessings we've been given, I come to realize that having a bigger house by way of expanding our home is probably just a little too much to hope for. *I haven't heard back for a few days, and that's OK. Our house seems big enough anyway. After all, there are a lot of people in this world that get along with a lot less.*

◆　◆　◆　◆

Those church meals that started to arrive on the very first week were meant to go on for three or four weeks, but in fact, they have been going on for three and a half months! The phone rings, and it's Kelly from Charco Construction. What follows is a whirlwind of thoughts and emotions.

Before I can mentally conceive of it, crews are arriving to extend the living room twenty feet to accommodate one more bedroom, making it a three-bedroom home. As the construction continues, the crew takes a liking to us, and we like them. They are taking the project *over the top*. We've ended up with one more bedroom, one more bathroom, an extended living room (which gives more room for the kids to play as they grow up), and a front porch deck where my new friend Cathy and I rock the babies almost every afternoon from 4 to 6 p.m. To top it off, they redo the siding so that it matches the rest of the exterior, and it looks lovely.

Larry is beginning to spend a few more hours daily at our music school, to keep it running smoothly. I am at home alone with two babies at the breast and two babies at the expressed milk bottles. The two at the breast are held in a sort of football position, one in each of my forearms. The other two are on the floor in infant seats with bottles, propped up with rolled-up towels positioned in their laps and at their cheeks, so the bottles won't roll out. I keep my bare feet handy and positioned near those in the infant seats in case they begin to list. I give smiles of reassurance and songs of comfort. I make a humble plea to them all to stay in place and cooperate, "because I just might not be able to help you if something, or someone, falls."

Up the hallway walks a worker, who is doing some finishing work and asks me a question about my preferences on some building materials. My jaw drops in embarrassment as he says in a completely nonplussed tone, "Don't worry, my wife is breastfeeding too."

Oh yeah, like I'm not embarrassed anymore.

It is a tad bit stressful to have construction crews around and about while caring for four infants. *Maybe it's just getting us ready for the near chaos we'll probably be living in for the next 18 years or so.*

11

EASING UP

It has only been a month since I last decided to push the breastfeeding regimen, but now I'm inclined to ease up on myself and my sons. I am going to allow more than one "bottle-only" feeding per day.

Our boys are ready in the kitchen, propped up in their baby seats awaiting a feeding. Larry and I are both at the ready, expressed breast milk bottles in hand, sitting in front of them with burp cloths over our shoulders. The infant seats are close together, so we can reach all of them easily. All the kids are hungry, so we get right to it, propping up the bottles with rolled-up diapers. Larry and I take the time to connect and visit while they suck away at their breakfast.

Chad gets a bit fussy in the tight quarters. He leans to the side, poking Kyle. Kyle starts to cry as the tension grows. Brett is looking at Dad, not interested in the conflict at all. I notice he's staring at Dad for a very long time. Something about that stare catches Ben's eye and he begins to stare at Dad as well.

Out of the corner of my eye, standing behind me, I notice that Larry has started his wiggle-and-sing coping mechanism. I turn a little further. There he stands, looking out the kitchen window, swaying back and forth with his burp cloth swaying right along with his rocking motion—back and forth, back and forth.

"Larry, look!"

"What?"

"Your sons—look at them. No, don't stop swinging the burping cloth. Keep it up. You're hypnotizing your sons."

We both bust out laughing, as I join in and we continue to swing the burp cloths rhythmically. As we sing and sway, we add some vocal effects to entertain ourselves. After fifteen minutes, every little guy has sucked in every last drop.

I am fairly taken with how the boys stare at that towel and track it back and forth, right and left, and then completely stop fussing. This will be our new standard way of calming them down when they are fussy. I'll stop short of calling it hypnotism, but it sure is calming!

I can't know what other people might think of our strategy. I'm always careful not to look up and make eye contact when I try it in public.

Opera—Bringing Instant Order Out of Chaos

The witching hours for different seasons may differ from parent to parent. For us, it's always between 4:00 and 6:00 p.m., especially as our tribe is now reaching the "arm-over-arm" crawling stage. Ben gets interested in a certain toy, so Kyle wants to have a look at it, so he grabs it. Brett plays with a music toy that makes him laugh, so Chad has to grab it and have a look. The whining begins, followed by crying, if not checked.

Now and then, I feel more like a referee than a mommy. Watching the referee in sporting events on TV, I'm often struck by what a thankless job it seems to be. Being in that position with my sons is a part of the parenting job I find to be fairly void of fulfillment. I remind myself that I'm growing character and good sportsmanship in my sons, as well as pleasant and caring dispositions. But sometimes it seems like the reality is that "survival of the fittest" rules the day.

I'm tired of the fussing tonight. I stomp my foot, push out my chest, open my mouth, and let loose with my highest and strongest operatic voice. I bring down the house with "O Sole Mio," then add, "O Mio del Sole," having no idea what those words mean or even if I have the right words. The boys just stop cold in their tracks and look at me, so I continue, making up nonsense words that rhyme. What a relief, to now have a tool by which I can instantly stop sibling rivalry—*Go, Sergeant Mommy.*

Larry walks out of the bathroom with a towel around his waist and joins in. Before long, instead of singing famous Italian opera excerpts, we morph into singing nonsensical conversations with each other in an operatic, comical style, complete with an operatic belly "ha-ha-ha" laugh.

Whereas the swinging towel had done the trick at three and four months, we now have something that maintains their attention for longer stretches as we sing. Wow, conversations with one another with absolutely no interruptions. It's bliss. But at ten minutes into it, I turn to look at our reflections in the living-room picture window. That is more than I can take. I drop to my knees laughing and drooling, all the while doing the potty dance. Larry mocks me with his rendition of my potty dance, and soon we are both rolling on the floor. The kids are enthralled, entertained even.

The next time we sing opera to break the fussing, we add hand gestures and extemporaneous choreography to ramp up the fun factor. Sometimes, just for shock value, we use that strategy in public—in small doses. It's a bit indulgent, I suppose, but we aren't quite grown-ups ourselves yet.

The main thing is that we're entertaining the kids and each other—and that's golden. It's one of the many tools that help get us through … day and night.

CRYFEST

Larry is finished at the music school for the evening. He walks through the door, perhaps anticipating that I'll be glad to see him, and that just maybe the boys will be asleep when he walks in. But I am a mess. We are all lying on the living-room floor. And we are all crying.

"Janna, honey, what's wrong? Are you OK?" he asks.

"No, I'm not OK—and I'm so very tired and exhausted all the time. I can't keep up this cheerfulness stuff without some quality sleep."

Dropping his briefcase, he comes over and lies on the floor with me, wrapping me in his arms. "We'll work this out, you'll see. It's going to be OK."

"But what can we do?" I ask in desperation. "It's not like we can ask other people to get up in the middle of the night and help us."

"I'll help you get everyone to bed. Then we can have a glass of wine and talk about it. Can we give that a try?"

"I'll try," I say through sniffles, tears, and lots of nose-blowing.

"That's my girl. You'll see."

I muster up an unconvincing smile.

After the kids are in bed, we sit and talk about it. The crying continues from their room.

"Your biggest problem is lack of sleep, right?" he asks.

"Yeah, I suppose. I can't even think straight about how to get everything done. I feel pretty much like a dried-out rubber band being stretched and pulled in four different directions most of the time."

"Here's a thought," he says. "At two and a half months, we gave them pacifiers, hoping it would help them fall asleep at night more easily, right?"

"But, no," I say sarcastically, "that would have been too easy. None of them made the effort."

"Yeah—every stupid pacifier model tried was spat out in disgust," he says. "And just last week, the same thing happened— our one more determined effort to get them to take the pacifiers. So, the crying in the night continues. But now that our babes are in cribs and no longer sleeping back-to-back with a brother in the same bassinet, each little guy has his very own space."

I nod. "And?"

"I've got a plan."

"What's that?"

"Let me surprise you."

◆ ◆ ◆ ◆

Today is the launch date of Larry's plan, a bold solution that he must know will be darn hard for me to agree to because he won't give me any hints ahead of time.

Our pediatrician has given us the benchmarks the boys needed to pass before they could be expected to sleep for six hours at night. They have all met those benchmarks. We know they are strong enough, healthy enough, and old enough to do it. But they don't seem to have the same take on it as we do. They've continued to wake us up all through the night anytime they want Dad's or Mom's company.

Larry starts to explain his plan. "Hear it out, promise?"

"Yes, I promise."

"Here's how we'll do it. We'll make sure they are all well-fed and double-diapered as usual. We'll get them all in their cribs. Then, we'll sing them a song or two. Next, we'll turn off the lights, and tell them they will need to sleep and stay in their cribs until daylight. Can you agree to that? I'll help you to be strong enough."

I nod tentatively. "OK, I'll try."

I am wavering in my confidence in our plan, yet I'm determined to give it a try. Everything is lined up according to what we agreed upon, but I am still uneasy about it.

We get them all in bed, sing, and encourage them according to the plan. We get in our bed and turn off the lights. Larry holds my hand firmly. He knows this will be very difficult for me, as my mother's heart prompts me to stay alert to cries and meet the needs of my babies in a timely manner. This will be a whole new transition for me. *I'm not sure I can handle it.*

We decide we will let them cry for up to thirty minutes if necessary, to give them a chance to fall asleep. After ten minutes, three of them are asleep. But it takes the last little guy the full thirty minutes of crying to let go and fall asleep. I cry right along with him. Larry holds on to me tightly, and we get past the crisis. Sure enough, they sleep through the night— well, for six hours anyway.

12

WHAT TIME IS DINNER?

It's time to start giving my sons pureed food along with Mom's milk now at four months. As I give it a go, I soon see that dealing with four babies lined up in their infant seats with their four spoons and all that tongue thrusting … well, it's a bit much. By round six of the routine, I am ready to minimize the hassle.

"Okay, guys, here's the deal. You are all exposed to the same germs anyway, so Mommy is going to go down the line with just one spoon. Got it? Good, here we go."

Maybe it will make it easier when the colds come around. They'll get it all at once and will be over it sooner. One spoon is the new standard, and that's that.

That helps, but it's not enough.

Just then, Mr. Fun-Time Daddy walks in the door, earlier than expected this evening.

"How did that one-spoon thing work out?" he asks.

"So much better," I say, "but not good enough yet. We can brainstorm later. Maybe you can play with the boys while I get us our dinner, eh?"

Every face lights up as Daddy starts his familiar routine of tossing, tapping, and tickling. He goes down the line tossing each guy's hands up, letting the hands fall down … up, down, then the whole arm, and finally their legs.

Next, they all get "rapid-tapped." Like someone typing with his fingertips, he taps their foreheads like they were keypads on a computer. Next, he does it on top of their heads, then the nape of the neck. The grand finale is, of course, the Wagner tickling tradition. "Goochy-goo."

Later, with all of our darlings settled in bed, we relax into our red wine unwind, as we reflect on the day.

"Did things go well at Wagner's today?" I query.

"Oh yeah. Man, the parents are so encouraging, all the time, every day."

I choke back my urge to say, "Must be nice."

He continues. "Just about every day someone goes on about how they just can't imagine how we do it."

"Yeah, I'm not sure how we do it either. But it just seems like things keep working out. Then something goes haywire and we figure out a different way to do things. I guess we just adapt as we go. What else can we do?"

I take another sip of wine. "So, along that line, Larry—recall what I said about the one-spoon deal not being quite good enough?"

"Oh yeah."

"Seems like they're not all getting hungry at the same time. Kind of like one of them thrusts the food out over and over. Then, when I think we're done, they finally get interested when all the others are finished. So, the feeding time just goes on forever. We need to tighten that up somehow. Got any ideas?"

"I so want to say yes, but honestly … I'm so tired that I don't think I could think clearly if my life depended on it."

"Can't blame you. I feel the same way myself. Want to veg out on TV?"

"Oh, thank you. I would love that."

During their nap the next day, I brainstorm about getting all the babies on the same schedule by using a math model. The idea seems quite logical for my mathematical mind, and I can hardly wait to run it by Larry.

I start the conversation with my math epiphany. "I've got it, honey. All we have to do is figure out the mean time for eating and work backward from there," I say with authority.

"Could you clarify for me what you're talking about?"

"Oh, sure. Brett usually gets hungry first. Right?"

"Go on, I'm listening," he says.

"I think maybe we can use the same logic as we did for the sleeping schedule."

"How's that?"

"OK, over the next few days, I'll pay close attention and chart the time between when the first guy gets hungry and the time the last guy gets hungry. I'll record the interval lengths. After three days of charting, I'll add up all the interval lengths. Then I'll divide that total by the number of feedings done over those days. That will give me the average length of the intervals. From that data, I'll have an idea of about how long to try and hold off the first boy that gets hungry, which will be one-half of the average interval, give or take, based on our intuition at the time."

"You really like this math stuff, don't you?"

"Yep, I do—makes me feel smart and empowered. So, when the first guy starts to fuss, we'll try to hold him off until we get to that mean time. Likewise, we'll be pushing the guys who aren't interested in eating to get going. Maybe we'll even put a tad bit of something yummy in their meal to get them going sooner than usual. Shall we give it a go?"

"Uh, sure, why not? Maybe you're on to something."

"Gee, thanks for the resounding vote of confidence."

On day four we are ready for liftoff. Ben starts fussing and clearly wants to eat. We pick him up, bounce him, cuddle him. We walk around the living room for as long as we can to hold him off. Soon, Chad starts fussing for food as well, and we do the same with him. Everything is set in its place and ready, lined up, and in order, depending on whether it's a *liquids* or *solids* meal. Today it's solids. Plans are in place for which two will be breastfed and which two will use the bottle to chase down the goodies. At the next feeding, when it gets to the point that we clearly can't hold them off any longer, and we are near the mean time, everyone eats. Per the plan, at first the ones who aren't quite hungry at the outset don't eat enough food to keep them satisfied over the next interval of non-feeding time. But as it evolves, they all begin to realize that feeding time is feeding time and *you'd better grab what you can, when you can.* It only takes me seven days to get them all on the same schedule.

Now that they can crawl, we decide to initiate a "fun factor" breakfast routine.

"OK, I've got the bottles and nursing gear ready to go, dear," I announce. "Go gather our guys at the end of the hallway. I will be at the opening to the kitchen with bottles, nursing gear, and burping pads in hand—kind of like a teacher's anticipatory set."

Larry goes in front of them, cheering and goading them on as they crawl forearm over forearm the entire length of the hallway and up into their infant seats. The two that are nursing climb right up into my lap.

"This isn't meant to be a race, babe."

"No," he says. "But it sure makes it more fun for me."

"Fair enough. We're always saying that parents have to figure out ways to entertain themselves as part of the deal."

"And we are the pros at that," he quips.

"One thing, though. If this parenting stuff is supposed to be so much fun, why is it I always have to change the poopy diapers?"

"Oh, that's because you're stronger than I am. I can't handle blood and I can't handle poopy diapers."

"Oh, brother, you are not very convincing," I say, shaking my head.

TV's got nothing on the entertainment value of watching your quadruplets crawl to breakfast. I wonder if anything is going on at this point in their little minds regarding the pecking order, or is it just hunger that motivates them? I can hardly wait till they're talking and sharing their thoughts with me.

WHO'S CRYING NOW?

Our Wagner quadruplets are the poster children representing the fourteen sets of parents greeted with the birth of quadruplets in the United States in 1981. It's January of 1982, and Gerber Baby Food Company presents us with matching outfits for use in this photo shoot—and even better, the promise of a six-month supply of baby food. Though we determined long ago not to dress Chad, Ben, Kyle and Brett alike, we decide in this particular case, it's appropriate to dress them in the clothes Gerber has chosen for them. We also decide they will all be smiling—but that part is apparently out of our control. We try in vain to get a row of smiles. At least one is crying every time. The best we get is a shot with just one crying, our usually smiley boy, Kyle. I think about the message we will send if the others are all smiles and Kyle is crying. He'll be dubbed the grumpy guy. A solution presents itself.

"Can we look at the proofs one more time?" I ask.

We look at the pictures again with an eye for a take where all are crying. There's just one. We settle on it, to be used for the publication, deciding that Dad and Mom will have to be the smiley ones.

SIBLING HIERARCHY—ORDER OF BIRTH

My nickname of *Sergeant Mommy* is well-earned. Someone has to figure out a way to bring some order to the chaos. There are feeding times with the observations and documenting of intake and volume, diapers to change, outings to pack for, clothes to have ready for the next day, and on and on. I grasp with both hands any strategy that seems to have the potential of increasing order, realizing we may not even know what order is for years to come.

The boys can all sit up and stay balanced on their own now. Larry is watching over them in our one full bathroom, all of them sitting shoulder to shoulder in the tub. They smile and giggle as they play with the bubbles and their rubber duckies.

I am in the kitchen, putting away leftovers from the yummy meatloaf dinner delivered this afternoon.

"Hey, Larry, how about this?"

"What?"

"You know how we put a little piece of paper with the boy's name on top of the clothes we have laid out for him for the next day?"

"Yeah, and that seems to work."

"Well, yes, but it's kind of tedious, and I have an idea that might work better."

"I'm hanging on your every word."

"Oh, cute. Is that why I called your name three times when you were in the same room with me before you answered? Anyway, how about just laying out clothes and every other thing in order of birth? As in Chad, Ben, Kyle, Brett."

"Heck yeah. Why didn't I think of that?"

"Because it's not your job. Remember, you're the fun guy that makes any one of us smile when we're crying. I'm the one that keeps things in order … well, sort of, anyway."

"Let's do it," he says. "Chad, Ben, Kyle, Brett, Chad, Ben, Kyle, Brett …" he chants, as he does a *Wagner Wiggles* dance until I've got the giggles.

We get everyone settled in for the night. As I get all the clothes lined up for morning by order of birth, he pours wine and looks for something fun on the TV.

Order of birth becomes the new norm for getting things organized.

After a few days of the routine, I wonder if there are times when Larry and I are rattling off the usual "Chad, Ben, Kyle, and Brett" when Kyle, Brett, or Ben thinks, "I'd sure like to hear my name listed first sometimes." *Maybe I should randomize the order or change it on a standard rotation so that each boy gets a chance to hear his name listed first.*

I get so wrapped up in the business of surviving each day, I wonder if I'll ever take the time to make that adjustment.

13

GOTTA GET OUT!

It is the third rainy day in a row, rare for San Diego, and I feel trapped, like a wild animal in a cage. *Where can I find relief? Think. Maybe an indoor mall? Sure, that will do it.*

Early on we were gifted with a uniquely designed stroller-bed. It has a rectangular base with high sides and an umbrella top. Our guys are so small that we can squeeze all four of them in—for another few weeks anyway. It's very cozy.

For the first few months, they seemed happy to be jammed in, close together. But by now they're getting a little bit squirmy, and this may be their last ride in this rig. Since it's the only way I can get them out and about without help from others, for now I'll have to make do with what we have.

◆　◆　◆　◆

Getting them ready and down to the car in the rain is going to take some domestic engineering with Larry gone. *They'll be up from their nap in about thirty minutes. I'd better get in gear.*

Grabbing the golf umbrella, diaper bag, rolled-up blankets for the stroller, four bottles of pre-expressed milk, snacks for me, four sets of extra clothes for my babes, and the car keys,

I skittle down the slippery terrace to get everything in order for a successful outing.

Running back up the terrace, I shake off the dripping umbrella, set the keys on the counter, and pick up the phone to let Larry know what I have in mind.

"Hey, honey, how are classes going?"

"Just fine. Are you OK?"

"Oh yeah, things are going just great."

"Really?" he responds, with some doubt in his voice.

"Yep. I'm so excited about what I have planned for this afternoon."

Giving him my optimistic "I can do this easy thing" rendition of the plan, I tell him everything will go smoothly.

"Promise me you'll ask for help if you hit a snag. And promise me you'll call the studio every hour to let me know you're okay."

"Promise. But I'd better get going, they're starting to wake."

To tighten the timeline, they've all had bottles in their swings while I've pulled myself together. Thirty minutes later they are cleaned up, changed, and double-diapered.

With two babes in my front carriers and two in the back carriers, I walk out the door with the umbrella doing its best to keep us all dry. I only need to make it the twenty feet to the sidewalk to unload my heavy load. *I'd better watch my step. I'm carrying all five of us down the steps in the rain at once.*

At the mall, I park the umbrella at one of the shops and start some power-walking laps, pushing my brood from one end of the mall to the other, snuggled up in their custom stroller. They get sleepier by the minute as I get more and more winded.

It's sheer bliss, as I finally feel the onset of the endorphin blast. I stop to take in the view. It's only now that I notice the onlookers. I'm torn. The idea of engaging in some adult conversation with another mom is enticing. Then again, I don't want it to turn into a scene. All of a sudden as I'm considering my options, I feel a brush on my arm. I turn my head just in time to see a lady bend down and pick up Chad from the stroller. So many things pass through my mind.

Is she going to grab him and run? How can I leave the other three kids if I have to catch her? Does she think her move is appropriate?

With these thoughts whirling in my head, I reach down and grab Chad from her.

My mama bear instincts kick in and I tersely declare, "Oh NO, don't touch my babies!"

She sharply replies, "If you don't want people to touch your babies, you shouldn't take them out in public."

Strangely, as I hear her rebuke, self-doubt makes its familiar entrance. I begin to feel ashamed. It takes me back to the all-too-familiar criticism I'd heard from my mom for not having done something quite right.

Why can't I be sure of myself? Is this a carryover of struggling to feel approved of as a kid? I guess Mom and Dad did the best they could with what they knew at the time. But I am so tired of second-guessing myself.

God, please help me to know what I'm supposed to do and then just do it.

I often find it a challenge to recover from *anyone's* criticism, even as an adult. For my part, I've made up my mind to express love, acceptance, and affirmation to our sons as they grow up, while simultaneously playing the role of a strict disciplinarian—a necessity with multiples. *I'll run the incident with the lady by Larry when I connect later tonight.*

◆　◆　◆　◆

"While I take it as a compliment that people are curious and care," I tell him, "it's entirely too exhausting to engage with each person that wants to ask questions. So, honey, I have an idea."

"Bring it on. What's your latest brainstorm?" he asks sincerely.

"I suppose everyone is curious, right? And they just want to ask some questions and get a feel for what our life is like, right?"

"Seems like it."

"So why not make a real cute flyer with a photo and a list of the answers to the most frequently asked questions?"

"Seriously?"

"Sure, it's a real win-win."

So we try it, and for the most part, it works beautifully. As soon as somebody approaches, I try to pin a smile on my face. Then I reach out, hand them the flyer with the answers to the most frequently asked questions, and as they read, we discreetly keep moving along, focusing our attention where it is needed, which is with our children. When the boys are old enough, they can hand out the flyers themselves. It will be cute and endearing to the onlookers. Here's the flyer:

QUAD FLYER

- Yes, we are quadruplets.

- Yes, our mommy is very tired and busy. That's why she made this flyer.

- We are all boys.

- Ben and Chad are identical, Brett and Kyle got their own egg.

- Our weight when we were born ranged from 3 pounds 11 ounces to 5 pounds 2 ounces.

- We were almost full term when we were born. Dr. Lapp says it's because Mommy and Daddy have good genes.

- OK, that's all for now. It's naptime. Bye-bye.

There Must Be a Better Way

This spoon-feeding stuff, with all the messy tongue thrusting, is driving me nuts. I don't get how those other moms put up with it. I guess it might be easier with just one or two babies—but still, there must be another way to get the job done.

Well-meaning friends drop off magazines about raising babies, but I seldom have time to look at them. On the rare occasion that I do pick one up, I fall asleep reading within a few minutes. But now I'm motivated—on a quest to find a solution to this conundrum. Perhaps I'll get ideas if I flip right to the back of the magazines, to the ad section.

There it is, exactly what I need, someone's little-known contraption called an infant feeder. I like the sound of that. Reading on, I find I can fill the cylindrical container with mashed-up fruits, vegetables, oatmeal, and the like. The kids can virtually feed themselves by holding the infant feeder and sucking the food in via an enlarged soft nipple with its large opening. It is like a baby bottle nipple, but softer and broader. The seal creates a vacuum in the cylinder as the nourishment is pulled into the infant's mouth, and the inside bottom section rises with each intake of food. It works kind of like a siphon valve.

Excited, I call the doctor's office. "Hi. This is Janna Wagner, the mom with the quadruplets."

"Oh, hi, Janna. How is it going? Are you managing okay?"

"It's one day at a time—or maybe more like one minute at a time, but it seems to be working out."

"Do you need to talk to the pediatrician?"

"Oh, that would be great."

"I'll get him for you."

After I tell him about my idea, trying to put it in a positive light, he pauses and says, "I strongly advise against it."

"Oh, why's that?" I say, as my spirits sink.

"Well, I'm concerned that the boys won't learn to chew and swallow correctly if you use those devices. I strongly advise against it," he repeats.

"Oh, I see. Well, thank you for taking the time to take my call."

I lie on the floor with my head in my hands, reflecting on all of the unique solutions we've come up with in our irregular situation.

Just last week I met a woman with twins. She said to me, "How do you do it? I'm just so overwhelmed and I only have two. You have four."

"Here's the thing," I say. "I believe that God will supply all of your needs, just as he has done for me. It's not that my job is harder or easier. That's not it. It's that, like my pastor says, 'God will give grace enough for the day and for your needs.' That's why I feel so sad when some husband points me out to his wife and says some inane thing like 'Don't complain, look at that lady—she has four.' In that circumstance, I think to myself that no one knows if the mom with one, two, or three babies might just be having an even more challenging time than the lady with quadruplets. Here's the deal. You were given twins, so God will equip you for just what you need if you trust him. He won't let you down. He may help you solve your challenges differently than you thought he would, but he knows what he's doing. Try to take confidence in that. I know it helps me."

As I reflect on that conversation, I am encouraged to follow my own advice. Not to be cocky and arrogant or disrespectful. But just to acknowledge that I've been given these four sons to care for and that I can trust my intuitions on how to best care for them, as long as I keep my mind open to his prompts.

Yep, infant feeders are going to become my new pal.

◆　◆　◆　◆

"Check this out, babe," I holler out to Larry from the kitchen, as he comes in the door after a full day at work. "They're all eating pureed peas, corn, and squash with their infant feeders. All I have to do is referee and clean up. Not bad, right?"

"Oh, yeah. If I didn't have an appetite before, I sure do now," he says, teasing me.

"I have an idea," I tell him.

"Oh no."

"Stop it," I chide. "Now listen to me. I bought two extra infant feeders in case the kids needed us to model it before they gave it a try—but it looks like they're all doing fine. Humor me, though, and agree to eat your dessert tonight with an infant feeder. We can all have our dessert together."

"Please tell me you're kidding."

"No. It will be fun. They'll be having applesauce, but you'll have your choice of applesauce or slightly softened ice cream. Don't say I never gave you a choice. You get to eat your spaghetti like an adult, but we'll eat dessert all together, and they won't know the difference. Sneaky, right? Maybe they'll think it's big guy stuff if Daddy and Mommy are doing it."

◆ ◆ ◆ ◆

We get Ben, Brett, Chad, and Kyle into their cribs after playtime, stories, prayers, love, and hugs.

"So, what do you think?"

"About what?" he asks.

"Well, I'm pretty excited to think we have discovered infant feeders. If that's not enough, when they go down for the night in their cribs, they stay down until the sun comes up. Those are two impressive accomplishments for kids who aren't even a year old yet, don't you think?"

"I'd probably be a lot more excited if I wasn't so tired," he says, yawning.

"Yeah, I get that. I'm tired too."

Umbrella Stroller Variation

Our whole tribe is headed to the La Jolla boardwalk. It's the same place Larry and I took walks with the boys in our front and back carriers before they could walk. This time we plan to push them in their strollers, letting them loose to run around later in the day on the lawn when we have our picnic.

I check to be sure that our custom double umbrella strollers are in the trunk. There are some manufactured twin strollers out there, but they fit neither our trunk nor our budget. Ours is one of a kind.

"How'd you manage to make them snap together?" I ask Larry.

"You know how policeman George hangs out in his tool shed across the street? I just went down there to pick his brain. He scratched his head for a minute, and said, 'All we need are four umbrella strollers and two strong, reliable clamps for each pair. We'll end up with two sets of twin strollers.' It's cheap and safe—plus, we figured you'd be able to manage it when you're out alone. And that's what we did. You gotta agree it makes it easier for you than lifting the shopping cart Gemco loaned us into and out of the trunk."

"Yep," I say. "The custom double stroller idea works great. The part about letting them run around on the lawn at picnic time is a little shaky. We need to work on that one."

"True that."

"Do you ever think back to that day, after my four-month checkup, when we thought we were going to have triplets?" He nods. "We were asked then if we wanted to consider *selective reduction*. Remember that?"

"Yes, and it gives me the creeps. We didn't even really think it was our choice to make."

"Sometimes, when I go in to check on them at night, I look at their faces and wonder what it would be like not to get to know any one of our little guys. I am so grateful that we both felt the same way when that option was suggested to us."

"On a cheerier note, got any ideas on how to rein in four toddlers in a park?"

"Not yet. I'll get back to you on that one," Larry says, as he runs off to grab Brett and Kyle, who have begun to run off in different directions.

The Very Next Sunday …

Since we've discovered the best retreat, bar none, is to the beach, where the negative ions bring out the giggles and smiles every time en masse, it's easy for us to get the motivation to pack up and go.

With beach gear in tow, we head to the beachside of La Jolla. Today we are going to attempt to maximize our beach experience with a new twist.

While I rest under the umbrella, Larry plays hard with the boys. I have to look away when he takes turns throwing them into the air and catching them just in time.

Chad decides to build a sandcastle with his little bucket as a mold. Nearby, Kyle is throwing sand at the seaweed and misses. It knocks part of Chad's sandcastle over, which as one might imagine sends Chad into a tizzy.

Ben starts running toward the water along with Brett, who is right behind. Larry rescues them just before the white water hits them.

All this and more as curious onlookers stare in amazement, trying to figure out if they are multiples. I thought I could rest, but I can't help but wish they were all corralled somehow where I could keep a close eye on them. I keep counting to four as my brood's antics take over an entire section of the beach.

Larry finally connects with me. "Do you want to come to play?"

"I think it's time for the Wagner twist idea," I proclaim.

Larry rounds up the boys like a sheepherder and brings them near. We lay out four towels, side by side, telling the boys it is nap time. Our little darlings lie down on their own special towel, with their hands at their sides. We put a lightweight towel over each boy so that it is dark, and we hope they will nap. It works. I get a full hour and a half of reprieve as they nap—the Wagner twist.

Quadruplets

14

SERGEANT MOMMY SQUARED

It's time to concentrate on figuring out how to get past this "terrible twos" thing.

It starts early for us, at about 20 months old. It begins with the occasional defiant turn of the head or ignoring one of us parents altogether, as well as pushing or aggravating a brother.

"This is not in keeping with the Sgt. Mommy code of ethics," I announce to my feisty foursome. *I'll have to check into the James Dobson parenting book on this.*

After some research, I say to Larry, "I think our boys need some very clear boundaries, paired with predictable and consistent consequences."

"Is that what the good doctor recommends?"

"That's my take on it. I think that meanness toward each other we've been seeing in them might be their feeble attempt at establishing a pecking order. But I bet they'll just keep going around in circles on that one."

Each little guy takes a stab at establishing himself as *in charge*. Each try is not accepted very well by the other three guys, since they're all the same age and none can really pull rank on their brothers. My mind goes to the military model of how the subordinates listen to the directions of their leader. I think through a series of possible scenarios. The troops become quite clear as to who is in charge in the military. They must follow immediately and with a good attitude.

Maybe I can take this Sgt. Mommy thing up a notch. Perhaps if they learn who's the real boss and that it's not any one of them, it will make it easier for them to respect each other.

We have apparently let my title of Sgt. Mommy slip a bit. So, with Larry's deep-voiced short instructions and my insistence, we reestablish a routine of giving not more than one short sentence. After they hear it, they repeat it, and then they respond with, "Yes, Sgt. Mommy."

"Larry, I'm amazed at how well this is working out, and it's great fun. Now you try it."

"Thanks, honey," he says. "I'm glad it's working well for you. But you know that thing about dads having an easier time getting respect just by using an authoritative, deeper voice when necessary?"

"Yeah, yeah, yeah, I get it. Life is so not fair sometimes. But here's the deal. I'm going to decide that my way is more fun than yours. Just let me live in my little fantasy world for a while, okay?"

Still, our kids drift back into defiance. It seems they're just not going to comply or cooperate until they experience a consequence.

CONSEQUENCES

I begin flipping through my parenting books and magazines.

Ergo, the first consequence, *time-out*. The offender must face the wall, keeping his hands to himself, waiting a prescribed amount of time before joining the tribe again. No lengthy explanations until the timer goes off. Reasoning and justifications before the consequence can undermine the process.

These are nuggets I'm picking up.

When I read that "a clever toddler can use his limited reasoning skills and cause parents to postpone, or even negate the consequence," I cringe. I've done that.

By the time they stand through a time-out and hear the timer click after two to three minutes, they've had time to reflect.

Next in line is the pinch on the shoulder next to one side of the neck. I also read this in my parenting book. Time-out is great, but there are times and settings when the lesson must be quick, certain, and without any confusion or negotiation. Through time-outs, we've taught our kids to stop on a dime if they are walking and one of us says sternly, "Stop." It can save bodily injury at one of those moments when a child breaks from the family and walks off in the other direction or starts to walk into a dangerous situation and needs to be stopped immediately.

Some situations require an immediate response even if it's not an emergency. Considerations that simply are best for the group as a whole, and in consideration of other people. Or, in our case, the very real possibility that one of us might just about be ready to blow.

So, in that scenario, we have developed the habit of putting our hand on our son's shoulder and quietly saying in his ear, "Consequences will follow." We've practiced this many times at home and they know that the consequence is a pinch on the shoulder, which is uncomfortable *but in no way harmful.*

Each boy understands the system well before we try it in a public place. The finger on their shoulder is the first clue. If they don't respond, they get a gentle verbal warning. If that still doesn't work, they get the pinch.

We've actually only had to use the pinch once or twice. It's knowing that it's a possibility that helps them to take charge of their voices and their behaviors. But, there is one deal-breaker. When one of us is driving a motor vehicle and the decibel level makes driving unsafe, we need a different method of commanding control immediately.

ENTER THE RED FLAG

When the red flag goes up, four boys freeze in place, even if they are three or four feet behind us in the van, and we have no eye contact. We've rehearsed the scenario a lot and it's become a game of speed, as in who can freeze and go silent the fastest. That 3 × 5-inch flag going up in the air rules the moment, and in an emergency, may save a life. When it's held up as a warning (as it is many a time), the boys always settle down quickly. Thankfully, raising quads has its perks. Multiples seem to learn well from the *consequences* that their brothers get. Lessons are quickly learned.

"TWINKLE LITTLE STAR" JINGLES

Along the line of safety, we must do all we can to be sure our children know our first and last name, address, and our phone numbers. Singing in operatic style was fun for getting control of chaos when we had four little babies, but isn't going to do the trick for toddlers memorizing a series of words and numbers. Simple is better for memorization purposes.

We've decided to make good use of each landing on our front stairs, stopping at each one as we practice singing addresses and phone numbers to the tune of "Twinkle, Twinkle, Little Star." We all sing together:

"We—all—know—that—God—loves—you, six—one—two—two—Brown—Lake—View!"

On the next landing, it's phone number time:

"We—are—all—a—gift—from—heaven, 4-6-4-7-8-7-7."

The amount of fussing and whining is inversely proportional to the amount of singing, so we keep them singing as long as possible. It keeps the fussing to a minimum and helps in memorizing important lessons.

STOP—A WORD THAT CAN SAVE A LIFE

Just when we think we have the *consequence* problems solved, it happens. Four cute boys are waiting patiently on the second step. All have passed the *address* and *phone-number* quiz flawlessly. As I turn to wipe noses and Larry turns his back for a split second to grab the gear, Brett stands up, starts walking down the last stair, crosses the sidewalk, and steps into the street—right between two parked cars. Larry yells "STOP!" in his deep, authoritative voice. But Brett just keeps on walking. Larry bolts and grabs him from behind, just as a car goes past in front of the two. It all happens in less time than it takes to wink. He's snatched back just in time to dodge the car. We all take deep breaths and I struggle to get my heart back into my chest.

After a stern scolding, we head to the park. "I can't believe Brett did that, honey. I mean, we just did the drill about the STOP word yesterday."

"I know. I still can hardly believe it actually happened."

"I guess it's one thing to teach them and have them know the rule, but quite a different thing to have them follow the rule without a moment's thought. Stop means stop, without any explanation. Somehow we have to convey that to them."

By the time we get to the park, we have resolved to shift our emphasis from playtime to safety training, under the guise of fun games at the park. Any riddle, rhyme, game, or song with the word STOP will be used to make the point. First up, a little preschool ditty:

I walk and I walk and I walk and I STOP.

I walk and I walk and I walk and I STOP.

I walk and I walk and I walk and I STOP.

Then I turn myself around.

Walk and Stop morphs into variations on the *I walk* part, such as "I hop and stop," "turn and stop," "skip and stop," etc. Next, we do any ditties we can think of that make listening fun. Our thought is to reward their listening with praise. This will increase their desire to pay attention a bit better. So, we invent different variations of Simon Says. I scratch a line ten feet in front of them.

Simon says take two steps forward.

Simon says hop three times.

Simon says touch your head.

Touch your toes three times. (If you touched your toes three times, but Simon had not said to do so, you had to go back three steps.) The first one to reach the line that had been scratched as the goal wins. So, praise for listening, points lost for acting without carefully listening first.

A 22-month-old child can only listen so long. So, it's time for another variation.

"Okay, guys, now listen very carefully. Here are the new rules for our new game. Can you be a good listener?"

All in unison proclaim, "Yes, Sgt. Mommy."

"In just a minute, I'm going to let you run around and play anything you want to."

"Can we go on the swings, Mommy?" asks Chad.

"Mommy said we can play anything, Chad," says Ben.

"I play sandbox, Mommy," Brett chimes in.

"I find roly-poly," Kyle says with a smile.

"Okay, here is what makes it very, very special," I say. "Daddy and I are going to give you prizes, so listen carefully."

"Candy, Mommy?" asks Kyle.

"Yes, raisin candies. You get three raisins squished together every time you win. When Daddy or Mommy says STOP, you stop right away. If you stop very quickly, you get a raisin candy."

Now they are all excited about listening and winning a prize. Along with praise, now they are getting a prize as well, since we find it to be a valuable reinforcement. And so the day goes, as we observe their listening skills and response time improving.

15

A REAL EYE-CATCHER

Grammy Jean, our neighbor who had given us the car, has helped us out of many a pickle. I love and admire her, and so do the boys. I think I'll run this one by her. I write in my diary, wondering if I'd ever take the time to finish the story after I run my new idea past her.

"Hi, Grammy. It's Janna."

"Good morning, honey."

"I've got the boys down for their nap, and I'm brainstorming on a new idea. Do you possibly have time to come over and be my sounding board?"

"Of course. I'll be right over."

Sitting on the sofa beside each other as the boys sleep soundly in the next room, I begin.

"Thanks for coming over, Jean. I've been thinking of how hard it is when I'm out in public with the kids and they all have to take ahold of one of my index fingers as we walk together in a cluster of five, with two guys on each side of me. They're so close to each other that they bump. It's all very awkward. And worse, they begin poking and provoking each other if we're out for long."

"But what choice do you have?" she asks.

"Have you ever seen a mother walking along with a child on an upper-body harness, like a dog on a leash?"

"I've seen that," she says with reserve.

"I know, I feel the same way. It just looks so cold and inhumane, like the child is pulling the mom along, doing the job of a sled dog pulling its master. The whole thing is just so distasteful."

"Is there more?" she asks.

"Well, yes, kind of ..."

"Go on."

"Yesterday I had some time to myself when Larry took the kids to Collier Park. I visited my favorite boutique store, Goodwill. There were these child harness setups hanging for sale for very little money. I thought to myself, *Hmm, I wonder if there is any merit to that method?* You see, there were a couple of times when one of them *did* let go of my finger. That got me thinking about the possibility of some crazy person grabbing one of my kids and running. What would I do? Leave the others and chase after that culprit? Scream for help? What if one of them drops my finger and runs into traffic? So, what do you think, Jean?"

She smiles, tips her head to the side, and says, "I think you bought the harnesses."

"Yes, all four of them."

"Well then, see how it works out. You'll never know until you try."

"Thanks. I just needed to run it by someone. When I try to imagine myself in public with four boys being walked like puppies, I can't help but imagine what people might think."

"Not everyone is going to understand your unique situation, Janna. But you can't control what others think. You'll have to focus on protecting the boys as the main priority."

"That's what I needed to hear, Jean!"

At the park the next day, I find myself filled with excitement and hope. *Eureka!* They love it! Now, instead of reaching up their arms to hold onto Mommy's finger and maneuver their way along the path without running into their brothers, they have a full three to four feet of freedom. It's great fun, and I know it's safer for them. All I need to do is just avoid eye contact so I don't have to be condescended to or feel like I need to explain.

I so yearn to be approved of and want people to think well of me. It takes a lot of nerve to use these harnesses, always wondering what people are thinking. On the rare occasions that I see another mom using them, I flash her a big smile and a nod of approval.

YOU'VE BEEN THERE?

What a treat to have another family with quadruplets visit! As a bonus, they have an older child as well. They are local, and their brood is made up of one girl and three boys, all the same age, and a sister, two years their elder. These quads are two years older than our kids and are excited about passing down their gently used clothes and toys. The nine kids in our two families run around in our terraced backyard, like a litter of puppies just let off their leashes, while the parents visit and share notes. After our kids are good and dirty, the older kids help our boys get in their bubble baths and get them all cleaned up. There is water flying everywhere. It's priceless. I take a mental snapshot of the scene and call it up whenever I need encouragement.

BRIGHT YELLOW WAGON

As I'm getting ready for my shower, Larry is getting the guys all settled into our bright yellow wagon. I begin to sink into the luxury of a quiet, hot shower, with nobody but me in the house, Larry is ramping up to pull four sons (in one wagon) the one mile to church. He encourages me to take my time and relax, and so I do.

If the kids get restless along the way, he tells them that they can play for a few minutes at Collier Park. The anticipation of playing at the park generally buys some patience and agreeable behavior.

Along the way, they sing Larry's original wagon theme song:

"Goin' to church in a bright yellow wagon,

Going to church on a bright sunny day.

Singin' God's praises in a bright yellow wagon,

Singin' hallelujah all the way."

Then Larry says, "Sing it, boys!" And they chirp out with their cute toddler voices:

"Ha-yay-you-ya in a bwite ye-woe wagon,

Ha-yay-you-ya on a bwite sunny day.

Singin' God's pway-zis in a bwite yew-woe wagon,

Singin' Ha-yay-you-ya all da way."

That pronunciation of "hallelujah" cracks me up every time.

I take my time, getting in the car to pick up the gang only when I'm good and ready, feeling fairly well put together. This

Sunday morning indulgence is a precious gift from my exceptionally considerate husband, and the boys love the chance to have Daddy all to themselves.

I catch up to them, we throw everything into the car, and drive the rest of the way to church. Once there, he drops off the five of us near the toddler childcare area and heads out to find a parking spot. That's when the gawking begins. They are familiar with the routine, and when I stick out my pointer and pinky fingers on both sides of my hips, they all grab onto one of them as we begin to shuffle forward.

Onlookers smile and tell them what good little boys they are. As they beam with pride, my chest is about to explode with joy and gratitude. As some of the attention begins to shift toward me, I am told what a great job I'm doing, even that it's an inspiration to others. At this moment, I know exactly what my purpose is, for now anyway, and I am bathing in the endorphin rush of the moment.

Thank you, Jesus. Help me to remember this moment—always.

As the service is about to wrap up, I squeeze Larry's hand, resting my head on his shoulder.

"What's wrong, honey? Why are you crying? Are you OK?" he whispers as he takes both of my hands in his.

"These are tears of joy, honey. I'm just so happy at this moment, so glad we got here today. It's such a hassle, and it's so easy not to want to take the time, but it pretty much always blows my mind when I hear Pastor Gregg talking to the congregation. I feel like he's speaking right to me."

"Awww, I love you. I'm glad we came too. Should we celebrate by going out for doughnuts?"

"Sure, babe. That's exactly what this moment calls for."

We take a few minutes to connect with friends from our Young Families class, then make our way to the toddler classroom to pick up our guys.

Kyle spots me as we get toward the beginning of the line and gives me a huge smile. We take time to express our extreme gratitude and ask the classroom attendant how they behaved. We get a positive report, without exception. But I think they just don't have the heart to remark about our guys' volume level. Whenever I turn toward the hallway of classrooms to pick them up after service, I can hear their loud shrieks above all the other kids. Happy shrieks, but definitely very loud.

Burnishing, in April of 1983

It's 6:30 p.m. on Thursday—Larry just got home and he's knocking on the door. I've just put the boys to sleep for the night. It's been one of those rare drizzly days in San Diego that makes me want to hunker down and cuddle until the sun goes down.

"Jan, can you open the door for me so I can keep these papers dry?" he asks as he drops his wet windbreaker on the outside porch and holds on to a bundle of papers wrapped in plastic.

"What do you have there? It looks like a real valuable treasure, the way you're holding it."

"It is. And I confess that I bought all this stuff on credit without running it by you. Sorry," he says, as he looks at me a bit sheepishly.

"Pony up. Let's see what you've got. Is it a stack of crisp $20 bills?"

"Sure. Don't you wish? Hey, honey, would you please wipe off the kitchen table for me? It needs to be super clean, not a smidgen of water or oil or anything."

"Okay, sure," I say as I walk around him and down the long hall to the kitchen, grabbing a dish towel along the way.

He spends the next hour telling me about the burnishing process he wants to use to create the masters for the music books he plans to publish.

"So let me get this right—you want to toss the curriculum books we've been using for the last seven years. Instead, you plan to create your own curriculum, with new lyrics and melodies. Right so far?"

"Yep," he answers with strong resolve.

"And you think we'll just figure out the illustrations along the way?"

He nods.

"I'm with you so far, but here's where I put on the brakes. You've also said that you want to drop the classroom setup from twelve students per class to eight students per class, and you think we'll end up with a better bottom line. That just doesn't make sense to me. I mean, I've spent years cold-calling and beating the bushes trying to get the classrooms full and bring in more revenue. How can minimizing class size improve the bottom line?"

"Work with me on this, Janna."

"I'll try."

"You'll really have to keep an open mind to see the logic of this. Can you do that?"

"I guess we're about to find out."

"Have you noticed that no matter how full we pack the classes, we end up having drops, and ultimately need to combine classes by consolidating two classes into one?"

"Yeah, that's a given."

"I'm proposing that if we have smaller classes, better connection with the parents, and a better knowledge of each kid in the class, that they might stay with the program a lot longer. We might be able to keep the classes packed at eight kids per class rather than twelve, and end up with fewer drops."

He turns toward me.

"You wouldn't have to make as many phone calls," he says.

"Now I'm listening."

"The new curriculum I have in mind will be custom designed for group piano with parent participation. We can make that parent guide we've been talking about for so long. There really isn't anything in the private lesson world that works for our eclectic, group-oriented format. I've given it a lot of thought and prayer and am determined to give it a go. Will you back me on this?"

"Wow, Larry, that's a stretch. I get the curriculum part, but, I mean, if you did a linear regression with the current data on reducing class size, the numbers might not pan out. ... But, because you are so cocksure of yourself on this, and because I believe in you, I will stand behind you."

"Really, honey? Thanks for believing in me."

He takes me into his arms. We fall onto the sofa, consummating our decision, and plan to start work in the morning.

◆　◆　◆　◆

Larry does the lion's share of the work and I join him in the evenings when the kids are in bed. We sit at the kitchen table with music staff paper, burnishing tools, and plastic vellum sheets of whole notes, half-notes, etc. It's a grueling and tedious endeavor in which one page often takes hours to prepare. The method is akin to using an iron-on patch with fabric. Only in this case, the vellum-backed note head is put face down on the music staff paper and the notes and rests are transferred with the burnishing tool held at just the right angle and rubbed back and forth until the symbol is transferred.

Larry is very exacting in his standards for this transferring of notes and symbols. More than once I proudly hand him a completed page, only to have him gently point out that "the stem on the third quarter note on the second line is not perfectly parallel to the first and second quarter notes."

"I'm sorry, honey," he says. "You'll have to do that page over."

"Argh," I growl under my breath.

Eventually, all four books are finished and published with plastic comb spiral bindings.

16

THE PARK AND THE LIBRARY

At Collier Park today, another mom is approaching me about my brood. She has twin girls and it seems like it might be fun to share. The girls are quite rough-and-tumble and can definitely keep up with my guys, who look to be a few months younger.

We are very comfortable and candid with each other. Nothing is taboo. We talk about diapers (she double-diapers too), discipline (we both use time-out), and finally, the frustration of getting the kids to eat healthy food (neither of us has a strategy for that one).

I notice a basket of toddler flipbooks beside her on the picnic blanket.

"Hey, we have some of the same books. Which ones do your girls like best?"

She grabs a couple to show me. "I check out a whole bunch every week at the library," she says.

"Really? You can check out more than one at a time?"

"Oh yeah. I usually get a whole bagful."

Just when I'm about to remark that I'd be afraid of losing track of the books and would have to pay late fees, she exclaims, "Do you go to the *Kids 'n' Me Storytime* at the library on Tuesday morning? It's free."

"Free, tell me more." *The time is flying by. We are chatting like a couple of old roommates.*

Glancing down at her watch, she jumps right up. "We're going to be late for a doctor's appointment. I've got to get going."

As she begins rounding up her girls and scrambling toward her van, I tell my boys, "Sit down, boys, right now, right where you are." There is a moment's hesitation in Ben's face, but he complies when he sees that I am serious about it.

I help my new friend, Jenny, get her gear in the van as she buckles her girls in.

Getting into the driver's seat, she hollers over her shoulder, "Maybe I'll see you at one of those Kids 'n' Me things, Janna."

"That would be great. Drive safely."

◆　◆　◆　◆

As soon as her van rounds the corner, I turn to my tribe and announce, "We are going on a field trip to the library." Lots of hoots and hollers of joy confirm that they are all-in.

The first thing on the agenda is to sign up for all of the toddler programs they have to offer. A friend of mine had once said to me that she believes you can find out anything you want to know from the public library. "No kidding, Janna," I remember her saying. "If they don't know the answer to your question, they will research it and find out for you. It's kind of like they have some code of honor about it or something."

I'm about ready to test that theory.

I remain hungry to learn every parenting skill I can, from any source I can get my hands on. It's clear to me that I'll only get this one chance to get parenting right. (Not only do we feel we have our quota of kids, but not long ago, Larry got the proverbial "We have enough kids" snip.)

We get to the library in a jiffy.

"Here we are, guys. As soon as Mommy gets you signed up for all the programs, I'm going to walk you over to the picture books and let you choose five books each to have for your very own for a whole week."

They explode into a cacophony of "Really, Mommy? I love you, Mommy." I go over the rules with them, which includes sitting still on their own stool, away from all their brothers.

"You'll need to read to yourself (which is really looking at pictures) while I talk to the librarian. If you can be good boys and follow those rules, I'll get you an ice cream cone when we are headed home."

After they're all settled with their books, I pull out the *quadruplet card*. I walk up to a female librarian who looks old enough to have kids, but young enough to be up with the latest parenting particulars.

"Excuse me. I'm here with my quadruplet sons. They're sitting right over there with the books they chose." I point, and her eyes bulge.

There is generally a barrage of curious questions that follow. But I know how long my boys will sit still. I must get right to the point.

"If you will be so kind, I wonder if you will help me find books for parents of toddlers? Then we can chat a little if they're not too restless later."

"Of course," she says, and we begin to look for books that will help my sons make better choices.

She is very kind, educated, and resourceful, and I get my books to pore over at home. We walk over to where the kids are sitting on their stools. But, of course, my two-year-old sons have a different version of staying on their stools. One is lying on it sideways, curled up in a ball, and trying to stay on the stool without falling as he rocks the stool back and forth. Or, like Chad, they are on the floor on their back, holding onto their stool, but definitely not on it.

"Oh no," I exclaim. "I'm afraid I'd better get the guys outside before they get any more restless." She didn't say so, but I'm pretty sure she was thinking the same thing.

I take them out for ice cream, not sure if they'd really earned it.

At home, my hunger for effective parenting ideas gets me skimming through the first book as soon as Larry takes over storytime. I get interrupted only for bedtime diapering and kisses.

PLAYTIME WITH A NEIGHBOR

When I get home from shopping alone, I run the groceries up to the front porch and walk two doors down to Grammy Jean's house to pick up the kids.

"Thanks, Grammy Jean, for letting my guys join Michelle on your patio for a while." Michelle lives in the house between ours and Grammy Jean's. It's nice that she's right around the boys' ages. "Did you have enough scooters to go around?" I query.

"Oh yes," she says. "Michelle got a new tricycle and was thrilled to be able to show the boys." As she speaks, I can hear the squeals of delight. The five of them are playing together, chasing each other around in circles on Jean's patio.

The kids know I'm here, but they keep playing. They are *that* comfortable at her place. After the hugs and *I love yous*, we start down the steps toward home, leaving Michelle to her solo gig as a circus rider on her new tricycle.

We run the twenty yards home, slowing to a walk as we make our way up the steep driveway to our front door.

Kyle's voice interrupts my thoughts. "Mommy, Michelle has a new twee-wheewer. Can I hab one?"

Before I have time to say, "maybe someday," I'm interrupted by three other voices saying, "Yes, Mommy, I want one too."

Hearing the plea from all, I'm overwhelmed and I answer, "When the cows come home, boys. When the cows come home."

"But when will the cows come home, Mommy?"

"I don't know, guys. Maybe we should watch out for them."

When we get back to our house, I ask them all to choose a book as I go to the bedroom to check the phone messages. As I come back out and turn to the living room, I see four cute kids, each with a book in their left arm, sitting on their knees in one of the living-room chairs, by the window, facing the view of the street below.

"What are you doing, my darlings?"

Ben turns his head over his right shoulder, saying, "I watch, see cows."

"Really?" I ask.

"Yes, Mommy." Chad chimes in. "I look window, I waiting the cows come home."

It's so sincere and so cute that I refrain from laughing and turn my back to get control of myself. As I look back at them holding onto their books looking out the window, watching for the cows to come home, I think, they are all focused, they are all quiet, and they are all sitting still. Maybe this watching-for-the-cows-to-come-home thing is a good idea.

TWO-YEAR-OLD BIRTHDAY (JULY 6, 1983)

Our boys will have a wonderful second birthday party at Dallas Park in La Mesa, with family and friends, once we finally get out the door.

I push Larry to get out the front door. "Come on, babe. Everyone's waiting for the guests of honor. Should I get the kids buckled into the van?"

"Sure," he says. "Give me five more minutes to pull everything together. I can lock up."

"Deal."

Grabbing a few extra diapers and rags for messes, I get the boys headed down to the curb, to get the show started. Five minutes later Larry gets all the gear loaded up and steps into the driver's seat, just as I'm buckling in birthday boy number four.

"Life is so much easier with our VW van, isn't it, honey?" I ask.

"Oh my gosh, yes! It might be old and out of style, but to me, it's as good as a stretch limousine."

"Speaking of limousines, I'm kind of glad we don't have all that publicity hoopla this year. How about you?" I ask.

"Agreed. I mean, don't get me wrong. I love the limelight, but in the end, it's you and me, family, and close friends that matter."

As he turns into an open parking spot, I turn my head to see if there is anything in the back seat that I should grab. It is empty except for one bottle-shaped item, wrapped in brown paper, that rolled out from under the driver's seat when he put the van in park.

That's odd. It almost looks like the way I've seen people wrap their booze as they exit the 7-11 store. But Larry wouldn't do that. He frequently assures me that he only drinks when we're at home together each evening, and then, only a small glass of wine. I choke my fear back down my throat, opting to wait until after the party to ask. *Anyway, it's just a beer. That's not a big deal.*

Grandma and Grandpa Magnuson give each of the boys their very own three-wheeler, just like Michelle's.

When Ben, the first boy to get his unwrapped, sees it, he turns and asks, "Did the cows come home?"

The foursome race around the 300-foot-long paved bike loop, competing in a bumper-tricycle game they've invented on the spot.

Just as bumper cars lose their interest, Ben calls out: "Hey, guys, guys, I go hill." He points to the steep, paved path that runs from the top of the parking lot to the quick sharp turn at the bottom. The rider must bank left at the end of the ride or run into a cluster of picnic tables.

I look at Larry as the boys huff and puff to get their three-wheelers up to the top, ready for the launch. He's reading my terror loud and clear, but just as clearly, he is not going to let me get away with saying, "No, that's for older kids."

We walk toward each other, me biting my tongue and him sporting his gorgeous, cocky, authoritative smile that communicates to me that I'm about to lose this battle.

"Honey, I know it makes you nervous, but this is what boys do."

"But they're not even boys yet. They're really just toddlers."

"Yes," he says, "but toddlers who have had an athletic, ruff-tuff first two years. They are ready for this. Scientifically speaking, the three-wheelers are bottom-heavy, so in fact, they are less likely to flip. And, I have Mel to spot them with me at the bottom of the hill—him on one side and me on the other."

"Okay, I guess I can handle it. But I'm going to be there too, to steer them away from the picnic tables if they get close."

"Good idea," he says, probably more to appease and calm me than anything else.

As I brace myself, something tells me that each year will find them going a little faster, being a little more aggressive … and a lot more terrifying for me.

THE TRUTH SHINES ITS FACE ONTO THE LIE

My pulse quickens and my heart sinks as I open the sliding door of the van. I intend to grab the wrapped bottle that I'd run across earlier, thinking to ask Larry about it. It's gone. When I climb in and reach under the driver's side, there it is. And there are three others, only much bigger. *What's going on. I don't get it.*

Thinking back to yesterday, when he'd offered to take the kids to the park while I got dressed, it begins to make sense.

What about all those other trips to the parks with the boys?

I know that he loves our boys with all his heart. And, they adore Dad. He is the fun-time guy, and they want to emulate all things Dad does and represents.

He's teaching them to be brave, smart, kind, obedient, and to enjoy life in general. But what else is going on during those trips to the park? Is alcohol another love pushing its way into his heart?

A still, small, gentle voice finds its way into my troubled, fearful heart. I am reminded of the many lessons we have experienced together in our Young Marrieds class at church. Tools for successful marriages were said to include love, respect, trust, kindness, forgiveness, and honesty. We learned that keeping secrets from each other could give distrust a foothold. It has a foothold in me now.

◆　　◆　　◆　　◆

We both find ourselves in the kitchen after the videos. "Hey, honey, today went great, didn't it?" Larry says with a smile.

"Sure did," I reply.

"How about I pour us some wine and we veg out in front of the tube for a while longer?" he asks.

"I'm not really in the mood for wine, but I'll meet you in the living room."

"Okay, it's a deal." He grabs an apple and tosses me one.

I walk into the room just as he reaches for the remote.

"Can we talk for a little bit?" I ask.

"You bet. Is everything okay?" he asks hesitatingly.

"I hope so." I sit down on the sofa beside him. My heart is racing, my face is flushed, and a tear comes to my eye. Mustering all my nerve and overriding the pounding in my chest, I calmly speak.

"I need you to tell me about the three big beer bottles that I found in the van today."

His expression goes flat as he looks away from me. He seems to be thinking about how to answer, and that frightens me.

Is he trying to put together an answer that sounds plausible, something that will quell my fears? Trust is falling out and escaping me like the sand in an hourglass. I just can't imagine how this is going to end well.

"How many did you say you found, Janna?"

"Why do you ask? Are there more?"

He drops his head, realizing his question has incriminated him. "Please, Larry, just tell me the truth. We can work this out together."

I picture Larry at the park on one of his frequent outings, the boys absorbed in play. *Does he reach into the ice chest, grab one of the quarts of Bud Light, put it in a brown bag, and spin it around a few times to conceal the contents? Is this in broad daylight? Is there ever an onlooker who takes note and wonders? Do any of the kids ask for some of his 'soda'?*

All of these questions are secondary to the real question: Is drinking a problem? And, if it's not a problem, why is it a secret? I feel disconnected.

As I wait, I continue to wonder. *Is he in a quandary of his own, wondering what I will make of all this and wishing, perhaps, that this would all just end and be forgotten?*

Finally, he ventures, "You know, Janna, beer and wine are really no big deal. It's not as if it's hard liquor or something."

"If it's not a big deal, then why did you try to keep it a secret?" That statement touches a nerve and his voice gets louder and more intense, on the edge of angry.

"I keep the alcohol under control," he says.

"How's that work out? What does that mean? Really, I'm sincere. Help me understand what it means to have your liquor under control."

"Every few months, I stop drinking altogether for a week or two, just to show myself that I have it under control, that it's not a problem."

"Why didn't you just tell me about the situation and your strategy?"

"I knew it might upset you, so I decided to just keep it to myself." He pauses. "How about this. I won't drink anything for the next week. You can check on me all you want. You'll see I have it under control."

"I'm willing to give it a try. But I'm not sure it's the right direction to go. After all, we've seen so many friends, band members, even members of our own extended families struggle with alcohol. I remember that in one of Pastor Gregg's sermons he concluded by saying that the best way to be sure you never become an alcoholic is to not take that first drink. Remember how he said that some people just don't manage their alcohol very well and don't know they have a problem until it's almost too late to reverse it? It's like some people are just wired that way. Maybe we should just stop right now before it becomes a problem."

"Let's try the one-week, no-drinking thing," he says, "and take it from there."

I agree, reluctantly, doubtful that things will end well.

17

THE BIG SURPRISE

I scramble up two terraces to the garage to gather our waterproof camping tarps.

"We are going to have a grand adventure," I holler as I walk the boys with my arms full.

Seeing the tarps, Brett ventures, "We go camp, Mommy?"

"This will be even more fun than camping, and you will have a chance to earn candy, lots of candy."

"Candy?" they all shout.

"Yep, candy. Want to get ready for the adventure?"

"Yes, Mommy. Me candy, I good."

"Me good boy too," says Ben.

"Well then, let's get ready."

Larry won't be home until after his evening classes, giving me plenty of time to get everything prepared for our big adventure.

As soon as Dad walks in at 7:30 p.m., I grab his coat and books and point down the hallway. "Go ahead and sit down at the table, honey. I dished up your spaghetti when I heard you walking up the steps."

"To what do I owe this honor?" he asks.

"I have a great surprise for you. You'll love it, and I'll show it to you as soon as you finish your dinner. Hurry up now, I can hardly wait."

As he finishes his dinner and walks back down the hallway to join me, a glass of wine in hand, I tell him it will all make sense when he sees what I have set up in the boys' room. So we tiptoe in, careful not to wake our brood, as I shine the flashlight onto the waterproof tarps laid out beside the four cribs.

"What's this all about, honey?"

"Remember how we've been talking about figuring a way to get the kids into preschool or some sort of organized playgroup? We agreed that they need to get a little bit better at their socialization skills."

"Yes, but what does that have to do with the tarps on the carpet?"

"Everything," I proclaim.

He looks at me, a bit incredulously.

"Do you want a hint?"

"Sure, I'll bite."

I run to our bedroom to get the bag of supplies I'd picked up at the thrift store with the boys earlier today. "Close your eyes now, honey. Be a sport," I say.

As he opens his eyes, he looks at me quizzically. "Are those miniature toilets you have lined up?"

"You got it! We're going to potty-train our boys tomorrow. I've got it all figured out. It's going to be great. We'll make it a competition. We'll take the four little potty seats and set them up in a row. Because your body has the right plumbing, you're going to show them how the deal works. Every boy wants to be like his daddy, so it should be a snap."

I have to admit that he isn't excited about using the porta-potty to demonstrate, but he's a great sport.

Just before he leaves for work, he does a demo. I can hear him from the other room.

"Now, boys, this is why Daddy doesn't need diapers. Here, let me show you …"

When he leaves for the music school, I proceed to take the diapers off the kids, cordoning off the house so that only waterproof surfaces are available for them to run around on. I let them know that the first one to pee in their porta-potty gets a candy. (Our version of candy is always a handful of raisins pressed together in a ball. To them, that's candy—at least for the time being.)

Within moments one of them sets the standard for his siblings. He gets to talk to Daddy on the phone and tell him that he's done it! He flaunts his candy in front of his brothers. In quick succession, the others follow suit. Since Larry can't be there in person to congratulate them, I pick up the phone cord, stretch it around to the nursery where the four porta-potties are lined up, and make a big show of calling him and raving about each new success. I take a picture of the child pointing to his accomplishment in the bowl so Dad will see it later, and I award each with the coveted raisin candy. By the time Larry comes home, each boy's contribution to their porta-potty is proudly exhibited by each one.

Two days later, the *Number 2* challenge starts to show progress, though it's harder to achieve. Within a few days, all four have figured it out. No more daytime diapers for this group.

DRY RUN

Subtle competition between siblings has made the potty-training of multiples much easier than I could have imagined. With them almost three years old, we are in a position to consider putting the kids in a morning preschool a couple of times a week. All systems are a go. That is, until I discover the price point for preschool.

Yikes, that's really out of our reach. I wonder if the preschool nearby in the Methodist church might be more reasonable? It's showtime, boys!

Wearing a fresh set of clothes, we go through a few dry runs, rehearsing good manners and behavior. It's time to load into the van, head to the Young Imaginations Preschool, and meet the director.

◆　◆　◆　◆

Thankfully, we are accepted and awarded a generous partial scholarship into the preschool. The kids have many opportunities for interaction and leadership. This life change is a milestone for Larry and me. *What will it be like to have a few hours each day to indulge ourselves?*

We are all thrilled, except for Chad. His separation anxiety breaks our hearts. Strength in numbers is no comfort to him when he sees us turn and begin to walk away.

He stops just short of crying, and anyone can tell he is making a valiant effort to be brave, but it is just painful for him to say goodbye. He finally turns his head and walks into the preschool to join the other kids.

We've learned a little bit about personality types along the way. We realize that Chad probably falls into the category of being a peacemaker, which is often accompanied by having a difficult time choosing, when given an option, and when separating from a well-known setting in favor of trying something new.

After a while, with the proximity of three family members there with him, he gets used to the goodbyes. Kyle, Brett, and Ben love all of the activities and settle in very quickly. Kyle in particular is thrilled to have an audience who can appreciate his special skill of doing a headstand for two minutes straight. Brett is always a favorite with the ladies given his sweet and agreeable demeanor, and stand-out smile. Ben finds lots of other little guys to chatter with and brings humor to the staff with the many stories he shares daily.

Huge Storm Brewing

On this New Year's Eve, 1984, I wonder how it's going to play out. *I wish so much I had somebody I could talk to about how I feel and what's on my mind. People say they admire me and Larry. I think they are taken away by him, as he is a real standout, and he lights up any room he walks into. There's probably nobody I know who realizes the depth of conflict we are in right now. Marriage is one of the best things on earth when it's at its pinnacle, but one of the most gut-wrenching things when there is conflict—and boy, do we have conflict.*

Should I call my mom and talk to her? No, on the day of our wedding she said, "Jan, don't ever come home without Larry being with you." I feel the door is closed to talk with her about any difficulty that might come my way. But I know what is going on, regardless of my belief that others would never believe the truth. So, I've been keeping it to myself—the knowledge of the increasing volume of alcohol being consumed. I smell it when he comes home from the music school. I notice empty bottles in the trash. Not just beer and wine, but small liquor bottles as well. Along with the alcohol comes a shorter fuse and the raising of voices that get us nowhere.

To share my enigma with another soul would no doubt seem unfair to Larry—a breach of trust. To share it with him would be fruitless. That whole stopping for a week goal came and went with him thinking he'd proven his point—that he can control his drinking. I'm convinced that he will not change his habits unless it is his choice to do so. For now, I will keep it to myself, draw my own line in the sand, and make some tough choices. The local Mummers New Year's parade is tomorrow. I'll put my energy into that.

"Hey, guys, gather around. Let me tell you about the parade you're going to be in. You'll be stars, and everyone will have fun trying to figure out who is who. You'll be a big hit and people might even clap for you. Shall we practice?"

"Yes, Mommy," they exclaim in unison.

"I make people smile and be happy," Kyle says with a grin.

"You're good at that, Kyle," I say, as I swallow the lump in my throat, wondering how things will turn out tomorrow, even imagining the worst.

"Let's practice on the sidewalk. You go down and sit on the bottom step. I'll get our bright yellow wagon from the back of the van."

As I make my way down with the wagon, I see that they're all deciding at once how to set up a parade route.

"Here's how we'll do it," I say. "Two boys on each side of our bright yellow wagon, with your feet dangling down, just like you sit when Daddy pulls you to church. And what should you do with your hands?"

Kyle and Brett glance at each other, no doubt deciding if they should do what they want to do—provoke each other and start a fight for position.

By some miracle, each of them decides to just be quietly active, swinging their feet back and forth and waving wildly at the imaginary parade onlookers. "Yep, that's exactly what you do, and you'll have some streamers and candy that you can toss out to the crowd. "I get candy too?" asks Ben.

"Oh yes, I'm sure you'll get lots of candy and have lots of fun."

"Daddy too?" asks Chad.

"Oh yes, I couldn't do this without Daddy's help. I just hope he gets home in time to get a good night's sleep. He's going to be up late playing a gig with Uncle Jon tonight, remember?

"Uncle Jon will drive back north where he lives." I point north. "Daddy will come home to be with us after the gig."

"I glad," Chad says, clapping his hands together wildly. "Daddy my best daddy in the whole world."

I push down my anxious thoughts, continuing to imagine the scenario in an unpleasant frame.

As time passes on this New Year's Eve, something doesn't feel quite right. *When Larry plays with his band, the time between finishing the gig, packing up his gear, and heading home has been growing a lot longer. Maybe there is more to it than I realize. Certainly, it's not another woman. Has alcohol become his mistress?*

I recall that broaching the subject of drinking touched a raw nerve with him the last time I brought it up. Of late, I've avoided the subject, for my own well-being. It seems as though it's a subject he considers to be off-limits.

But what about this?—I've never even once seen him tipsy. For a fleeting moment, this thought calms me. *But it comes back to this: the frequency of that mistress continues to increase, while our time together decreases. It's a habit that's growing, an unwelcome guest, one that threatens our intimacy and trust in each other.*

I fear that the kids will eventually discern the conflict. Daddy is their hero, and they want to do everything that he does. This is one behavior I'm determined that we will not pass on to the next generation.

Maybe Larry's grandma Claire was right. Maybe alcohol truly is a poison, at least for some.

One thing I know for sure. No one will believe me if I tell them there might be a problem. I'm pretty sure they would just laugh at me and say, "You're worrying about nothing, Janna."

◆ ◆ ◆ ◆

Larry is in the last set of his five-hour gig by now. The kids are all sleeping soundly.

Just as I check to be sure I have everything in line for the parade, Larry calls to connect, to say "Happy New Year," as he does every year, right after the band plays "Auld Lang Syne." He sounds fine. For now, I just have to wait and pray that this New Year's Eve has a happy ending.

We had talked about staying sober and safe, together decided that he would have a glass with soda on the piano. People would figure he had a drink already and be less likely to do the classic

"Here's a drink for the piano man" thing. He's agreed to come home right away when the gig ends at midnight, because of the parade we are scheduled to lead in the morning.

Soon it's 1 a.m. Then 2 a.m. And finally, 3 a.m. when he comes tiptoeing in the door, and there's that telltale smell. I pretend to be asleep to avoid conflict. When he is soundly sleeping, I get up and prepare for my alternate plan.

Something has to change; what it is I'm not sure. All that is certain in my mind is the option I had decided on if New Year's morning unfolded this way.

I will leave in the morning with the boys. I have all the security of a tank of gas, a credit card with a $500 limit, and all the groceries I've transferred from the kitchen to the van. I plan to drive the group home to my roots in Seattle, regardless of what Mom said years ago. Larry doesn't know my intentions and I have *not* thrown down the gauntlet with any ultimatums. From my experience so far, those don't help.

"Time to wake up, my darlings," I say. "We have a big day ahead of us."

Larry is sleeping it off, and the boys are in their high chairs, eating what may very well be their last meal in this, their first home. Just as I begin taking off their bibs, thinking we'll jump into the already packed van before Larry even wakes, Kyle looks up and smiles at something in the hallway.

I turn my head. "What is it, sweetie?"

There, outside our bedroom door, stands Larry. I brace for conflict, taking a deep breath to still my racing heart. Even before he speaks, I am brainstorming an alternative exit strategy, reminding myself not to respond to any angry words that might arise. But this does not unfold as I anticipate.

He makes his way down the hallway to the kitchen where we are.

There is a transparency in him that I've never seen before. *What is happening? I'm confused.*

He looks at me, drops his chin, and to my astonishment, kneels. Looking up at me, he takes a slow breath, and without wavering says, "I have a problem."

PART THREE

18

PROGRESS

January 1, 1985, marks the first day of my precious husband's sobriety. When Sunday comes around, Larry surrenders his problem to God and says he can no longer drink. Not even a sip.

"Is there anything I can do to help with this life change?" I ask.

"It would help a lot if you didn't drink as well."

Interestingly, I feel some resistance.

"I'll make that commitment with you, babe," I finally blurt out. "Let's do it together."

SMALL GROUP

New resolutions are easy to proclaim, but harder to fulfill. That's been my experience. *We settle on vowing to live life with a clean slate, without secrets from one another. We'd failed at that before, so what will ensure our success this time around?*

Larry is watching the Super Bowl game between the San Francisco 49ers and the Miami Dolphins and drinking hot chocolate while I enjoy watching the sideshow of four little boys taking down the unbreakable Christmas decorations.

Larry has his attention wholly on the game when I experience an aha moment. Venturing out on a limb, I say, "Hey, babe, remember that announcement last week in church encouraging us all to join a small group of like-minded, similar-aged people?"

"What's that, Jan? I was watching the replay."

"Never mind, I'll catch you later."

Eventually, we are all in the kitchen, munching down nacho cheese chips. I bring it up again. "Is my timing better now?" I ask.

"For what?" he asks.

"To bring up a small group."

"Oh yeah. I'm listening now."

"So, honey, Kevin and Kelly from the Young Families group invited us to join a group at their house. It meets once a week. They share a topic, eat lots of food, and have lots of laughs together. Relevant family topics are discussed from a faith-based perspective. What do you think?"

"I'm not averse to the idea, but I think it would be a real hassle to get our kids fed, ready for bed, and then take them over to someone else's house for an event that doesn't end until after their bedtime."

"Good point. Here's a thought. How about having it at our house? It would pretty much guarantee our participation each week, wouldn't it?"

"But there's no way we could get the kids settled down before our friends arrive. So how would that work out, Jan?"

"Maybe Grammy Jean would be willing to help. We could get the kids all ready for bed, walk them down to Grammy

Jean's in their jammies, let them go to sleep there, and then after the meeting, you and the other men can carry them each home and get them in their beds—a real win-win, don't you think?"

"I could do that. I think it would be pretty fun."

"I love you, Mr. Wagner," I exclaim, sealing my appreciation with a seductive kiss.

MOONLIGHTING

Sometimes with a family-owned business, the coffers run dry and the owners must take desperate measures to keep it afloat—the famine part of "feast or famine." Such is our immediate situation with Wagner's School of Music. The period of 1985–86 has had its high moments but finds us with funds running dangerously low.

It's the third of the month, and time to tally up the parent tuition payments so I can pay the bills. With Larry watching the boys, I retreat to my garage office to do the accounting.

As I begin crunching the numbers, it becomes clear that the income falls far too short to cover the bills, which are due by the eighth of the month. I've entered the payments into the ledger books. Grabbing a stack of envelopes, I address reminders to those whose invoices are still outstanding. There are about 25 parents who are late.

For the next few days, it's a nail-biting experience waiting for all the payments to come in. When the eighth of the month comes, everything is covered, but I am an emotional wreck.

"Honey," I say, "what do you think about this month-to-month mess we're in? Is there anything we can do to climb out of this rut?"

"Well," he says, "our friend Jim throws papers for the *Union-Tribune*. He works the graveyard shift. He says there is a job opening—and I did have a paper route once when I was a kid. It might get us over the hump until I get more gigs and we enroll more students."

"Are you considering taking a paper route now, at this stage in your life? I mean, you can't have the parents of the music school see you going around on a paper route. That would be embarrassing, demeaning, and make it look like we're going out of business, maybe even making things worse than they already are."

"That's what I was thinking too. But the fact that the newspaper doesn't get delivered in the middle of the day, but during a graveyard shift, makes it possible. I mean, it's the middle of the night; no one will be checking to see who's delivering their paper."

"But still, somebody from the music school or the neighborhood just might see you. That would be too weird."

"How about this. I'll take a route that's far from our school and our neighborhood. I think maybe they just throw the papers out of the car window and onto the porch. I can see that working out. I can even make a sport of it."

"You'd do that?"

"I don't really think we have any other options. Besides, it's temporary, right?"

He's doing it. The co-owner of Wagner's School of Music commits to a paper route for six months to get us over the hump. During that time each of our sons takes a few turns throwing papers with Daddy in the middle of the night, topped off with a visit to the doughnut store on the way home. They think it's great fun and get a chance to see the work ethic in action. On Brett's third turn for a paper-throwing adventure with Daddy, the rest of us are all cuddled in bed, fast asleep.

Wise Counsel

As we make installment payments to Agnes and Paul, the couple who sold us the original music school, we are late more than once.

"Don't worry, Janna," Agnes says to me over the phone. "We understand. You'll catch up later, we know. We wouldn't have sold it to anybody else but you guys, no matter what our financial advisor might have said."

That relieves my angst for a moment. Then my eyes drop down to the stack of mail piled on my desk.

As I open the first envelope with dread, I'm surprised to see a credit card with our names on it.

"Look at this, Larry. We are being offered a $500 line of credit for just a 20% interest payment per annum. It says we only need to make a small minimum payment monthly."

"Let's jump on it," he says. "This could save our credit rating and our behinds."

What's more, I discover our credit score is just high enough to qualify for a few more companies to extend cards to us with $500 limits.

I like the sound of that word "qualify." It makes me feel like I'm upscale and worthy of trust.

We say yes to all of the offers. Balances due keep mounting as we make the minimum payments each month.

Like a locomotive train that is quietly approaching, with its roaring engine pushing the cars forward from behind, we sense danger closing in on us. *Are we falling into some kind of credit card trap? The balance barely moves with each payment.*

Now, we have a $15,000 balance on our cards.

How will we ever dig our way out of this mess?

As the kids and I head over to the stationery store to stock up on achievement stickers for the school, I hear an advertisement that catches my attention.

"Quiet, guys, right now. I need to hear this."

I turn up the radio. "CCC, *Consumer Credit Counselors,* is a nonprofit organization that works with individuals and creditors to negotiate lowered monthly payments for their clients," the ad begins.

I make a mental note to call them as soon as we get home and I have the kids settled. *I can hardly wait to share this with Larry.*

◆　◆　◆　◆

After I get off the phone with CCC, I feel light-headed. I call Larry, barely able to contain my excitement.

"Larry, the goal is to destroy all credit cards, in return for making lowered payments toward the current balance due until the balances are paid off. The money comes right out of our account."

"Go on."

"The monthly payment would be about $230. They do all of the negotiating with our creditors, and the phone calls and bills stop immediately. All of the interest stops too."

"What about our credit rating?"

"There's no way around that being affected. It will be bad for about three years but eventually drop off the map. The good thing is that our payments will show good faith.

"We'll have to attend a couple of classes they lead on budgeting topics. Should I make an appointment for us?"

"Definitely. The sooner the better."

◆　◆　◆　◆

We begin to get out of debt. But I realize that money is not our only problem. There is a growing disconnect between us—a chasm—and it is getting wider.

"Larry, could you go ahead and take the trash down to the street now?"

"I told you I'd do it. I just don't want to do it right now."

"But they pick up the trash tomorrow morning."

"Yes, Janna. I told you I'd bring it down, didn't I? I'm into this show, so I'll get the trash when there is a commercial."

"I hope you remember it this time."

The volume goes up a click, then another. Having a softer, female voice by nature, I feel bullied, like I'm being yelled at.

"Just put the stuff on a list, would you, and give me a little room to breathe. I always get this stuff done eventually."

"You said you'd get milk too, and you forgot that."

"Really, Janna, a gallon of milk? Are you going to make a big deal about that? OK, fine."

He jumps up, puts on his shoes, and grabs the car keys without looking at me.

"You don't have to get it now. I can manage without it. I just want to know that we'll have some by tomorrow."

"Well, you've ruined my downtime already, so what's it matter? Forget my show, this gallon of milk is more important. I asked you to put my favorite shirt in the wash yesterday and you forgot too. What about that? Or is it just my mistakes that you take notice of?"

"Oh, Larry," I say. "I'm sorry about that."

"I'll grab the milk, but I think I'll go to the music school and work with my new song for a while. If you're asleep when I get back, I'll just sleep on the sofa."

And he walks out the door, slamming it behind him.

I'm angry, disappointed, and sad—and I can hardly even remember what we were arguing about. All I know is, I miss my husband.

◆　◆　◆　◆

The next morning both of us are tucked in. Not confronting, but not embracing either. An hour before I know he needs to leave for work, I muster up the nerve to ask him about counseling.

"Honey, I found out that there's a counseling center that's right on the way to the music school."

"What are you talking about?" he asks. "You mean you talked to someone else about our problems?"

"No, no, I told them I have a friend that needs some help."

"You go ahead, but I don't need it," he says. "I've got to go. I'll see you after classes."

Hmm, not the response I was hoping for.

When the boys are napping, I put in a call to the counseling center. I lead with, "May I speak to you confidentially?"

"Certainly," the receptionist replies.

"I'm the lady in La Mesa that has the four-year-old quadruplets, and I'm having a little difficulty. Is there someone I can talk to?"

Within a couple of minutes, a man comes to the phone. "Hello, Mrs. Wagner, this is Gordon Bear, the senior associate. What can I do to help you?"

As I open my mouth to speak, I burst out crying. Finally, when I get control of myself, I explain that Larry and I are having trouble communicating, raising our voices a lot. He suggests that I come in tomorrow, saying there is an opening at the end of the normally scheduled appointments, at 6 p.m.

"Grammy Jean will probably watch the kids for an hour if I can talk my husband into coming."

"Well," he says, "here's what I suggest. Let your husband know that you want to learn to handle conflict and that you think maybe you can improve your skills with some help. Let him know that you'd appreciate his support. He may surprise you and join you. If not, you will have set the right tone."

Two Months Later

Now that Larry is on board with the counseling sessions, we make better progress.

In one of my counseling phone calls, I practice with Gordon.

"I think I hear him saying that he doesn't want me to ask ..."

"I'm going to stop you for just a moment, Janna," Gordon says.

"Oh, did I mess it up?"

"No," he says. "We just need to tweak it a bit."

He reminds me that I need to look right at Larry, talk directly to him as if no one else is in the room. The whole point of the exercise is to listen carefully enough that I can fairly accurately summarize and say back to him what he said, without making any judgments, checking with him for accuracy along the way.

It seems like a pretty elaborate way to communicate, but I admit to myself, *It helps me to concentrate on the issue at hand without getting worked up emotionally, assigning blame, or losing my temper.* I take the directions seriously and give it my best shot at every session, carrying through at home as we talk about touchy issues.

Larry doesn't seem to be convinced that it's worth the effort yet, and often just jumps right into a conflictual conversation. I remind him of the steps we agreed to take. And the volume-up clicks begin. I try to stay calm.

"I thought we were going to follow the pattern Gordon taught us in counseling." … Click.

"I just went along with it, but I think it's unnecessary," he says emphatically. … Click.

"Why didn't you say something during our session?" I challenge. … Click.

"You would have disagreed."

I go up another click to match his volume. "You can't tell me what I *would* have done."

"Oh, please, are you going to tell me you wouldn't have gotten mad?"

"Well, it does make me mad. You make me mad. You're always making promises that you don't keep."

"Oh, really? Name one. Go ahead, name one," he says, leaning forward.

I pause to reflect.

"See," he interrupts. "You can't even remember."

A click, and tears. "I don't even remember what we're arguing about right now. I am just so angry and frustrated. You make me so mad." I stomp out of the room to throw myself down on my pillow and cry.

That's the path our arguments tend to take, and we get nowhere except mad, frustrated, and polarized.

At our next counseling session, Gordon reminds us both that we can each only have control over our own attitudes and behaviors. We are both powerless to change each other.

"Practice staying calm," he says. "Find what helps you to do that. Maybe a silent prayer, maybe counting backward in your head from ten, maybe a cleansing breath. Find what works for you. Practice it. Then use it. Remind yourself that you are responsible for your own stuff. That's all you can have control over."

He tries to get us on track, but it's a challenge. Over the months, he instills in me some fundamental truths. One is that Larry can't make me mad. Things he says or does can only make me mad if I allow them to. I usually allow them to. I have such a drive to resolve disagreements, and so does he. Larry and I both are gaining valuable skills during counseling.

We are so good together when we're in sync. It's like there are chemicals in the air that spark our exchanges, humor, and playfulness. He's my favorite person to be with, anytime, anywhere—until there is a conflict. Then each of us seems compelled to convince the other of our own point of view.

◆　◆　◆　◆

"I'm home," I holler, as I walk in the front door following one of the parent meetings which I lead at the music school.

"Hi, darling," Larry says sweetly.

Turning off the porch light and locking the door, I ask, "Did the kids go down okay for you?"

"Yep. We did the four-in-the-tub-at-once routine, then stories, prayers, and a bit of a *Bugs Bunny* video to top it off. Now I'm all yours, babe."

"Bugs Bunny's your favorite, right?"

"Well, yeah, but they liked it too."

"How generous of you," I quip.

"I told them Mom would be so proud if I could tell her they'd all gone right to bed and right to sleep. That did it for them. They were asleep within about four minutes."

He grabs my briefcase and coat and leads me to the sofa to sit down.

He takes off my shoes and begins to massage my feet. As he moves up toward my thighs, I am almost completely relaxed and aroused; my skin begins to tingle.

"I have to admit something," he says softly.

"Oh, what's that?"

"The counseling is helping our relationship so much."

"Show me."

19

A CALL FROM THE GODFATHER

"OK, guys," I say. "I need you to be quiet in 5, 4, 3, 2, 1. I'm going to take this call. Who can be the quietest? Here I go."

"Oh, hi, Uncle Mel." (Mel is not only a local jazz star, playing solo and ensemble gigs, but he's also been a good friend of ours since college. He's been a perfect choice for godfather.) "The boys are gonna be so excited that you called. Should I get them on the phone with you?"

"No. Actually, Janna, it's you I wanted to talk to."

"What's on your mind."

"What's it looking like these days with the casual gigs that Larry does alone, or together with you?"

"Funny that you should ask. I was just thinking about how nice it would be if we didn't have to spend, or at least Larry didn't have to spend as much time away from the boys doing gigs. I've already pulled out of playing nearly all of the casuals with him, but he's still at it. I mean, it's great money and all, but in about a year from now, the kids are going to be in elementary school every day. If Larry's still working weekends, it's going to cut out on a lot of the family time. I've been brainstorming on a work-around for that one. Any ideas?"

"You still play your flute, right?"

"Oh yeah, all the time around the house, and occasionally on gigs with Larry. You know, as the Piano-Flute Duo, but nothing like we used to do before we had four sons."

"Have you ever been to the Crown Room at Hotel del Coronado?" Mel asks.

"Oh, sure! We eat lunch there all the time," I say, laughing. "Not."

"This might just be perfect."

"What are you talking about?"

"I heard through the grapevine that they are looking for something sharp, original, and classy for their Friday and Saturday evening dinners. I heard something about the hours being like 6 to 9 p.m. on Friday and Saturday evenings every weekend. Would that interest you guys at all?"

"Are you kidding? Well, the boys go down to bed at 6:30 and the commute would be maybe 30–40 minutes to the hotel. We'd only be missing an hour or two of awake time with the kids if we could work it out with Grammy Jean."

"Hold on, don't get ahead of yourself just yet. There is an audition for the gig."

"Wow, Uncle Mel, you are our favorite musical godfather," I exclaim. "Tell me about the auditions."

Yet again, someone was watching out for us. We had been to the Hotel Del many times to do wedding gigs in the courtyard, nestled up near the shoreline on Coronado Island.

Even pre-kids, we'd gone to the Del to see the stunning display of holiday decorations at Christmastime. As newlyweds, we had rented bicycles and trekked around the island, dreaming of what it might be like to actually live in one of the many highbrow homes by the resort, no two of them alike. One sunny summer day, when the boys were three, we took them there to play in the public beach area on the fringes of the resort. We had poked our heads into the Crown Room restaurant to get a sneak peek at the opulence of the room. It had been built in 1888 of solid wood, made to look like an inverted, magnificent ship. Its frame soars up from the floor some thirty-three feet to the tip of the curved ceiling. We had never dreamed of stepping into the room, let alone eating a meal there. The idea of playing on the main platform at the grand piano had never occurred to us. Uncle Mel, with his many musician contacts, opens this door for us.

We opt to play a cross-section of classical, pop, and show tunes for the audition. Larry Lawrence, the owner of the hotel, likes us, and we will start playing there every Friday and Saturday evening. First, we'll have to dress the part.

I find an outlet store that sells evening gowns at a discount, and Larry insists that he only needs one tux. Grammy Jean agrees to get the kids in bed in our absence. And as I had predicted, we are only missing out on about an hour or two of "awake time" with the boys each night. It's ideal.

The acoustics for the flute and grand piano are magnificent. We are very well received, and it is fun to see the occasional movie stars and dignitaries dining there as we play. We don't ever have a meal there, but it is a delight to play a steady gig in an atmosphere where we are appreciated and pretty much never have a concern about the occasional drunken folks coming up to slur a list of requests for us. This gig is a sheer delight in comparison to some of those kinds of gigs in the past.

On the way home, we often stop to fill the tank or go to the grocery store to stock up, going up and down the aisle, dressed to the nines with gown and tux. That must look weird to the other shoppers. We just go about our business, leaving the onlookers to wonder. It makes late-night shopping an adventure rather than a chore.

A Dream of My Own

Over the last five and a half years, I've felt like I could hardly come up for air.

Suzanne, my college roommate, was just here from Seattle for a visit. She was a sport, thinking nothing of it when she discovered her guest room would be a small corner of the playroom downstairs. The boys loved goofing around and climbing all over her, showing off and in general doing whatever they could to get her full attention.

On her last night here, we hunkered down in the living room while Daddy got the kids all tucked in.

"So how are things going for you, Janna?"

"Well, it's ironic. Finally, with my darlings in school five days a week, I think I may be able to breathe and relax a bit—but I just don't seem to be able to settle down. My brain just keeps spinning. I know that a driven woman with time on her hands can be a dangerous thing. Is that me?"

"If the shoe fits. But really, Janna, what are you scheming?"

"Maybe I have Charco Construction to thank for this newly birthed jag I have."

"How so?" she asks.

"Remember how they came in and expanded our house? They even matched the old cedar siding. It looks like it was designed that way from the beginning. I can't believe the transformation."

"And … that makes you think of what?"

"Well, now that I have time to take a breath and look up, I realize that people with imagination and skill can really change a home if they have the right vision."

"Something tells me you have a vision. Go ahead, lay it out there."

"OK then. See that quilt you have wrapped all around you? Well, of course, it didn't start out with all those designs in it. First came the idea, then the color choices, which drove me to go to the quilt shop to gather the supplies."

"Uh-huh."

"When I got home, I had to cut the fabrics, place them where they belong, sew them together, add the batting, and secure all the edges. And there you are snuggled up in it. It's a quilty thing. I think construction is similar to quilting—it's just with a different medium."

"It's a bit of a stretch, Janna, but I get it."

"Those builders demonstrated right before my very eyes what could be done with some vision and construction skills. I'm brainstorming on how to make our house more functional. But neither Larry nor I have much knowledge of building design. Possibility thinking is all the rage in the 1980s, right? I think I've caught the bug. The problem is how to put my construction ideas on paper."

"Are you talking about adding on?"

"Yes. Exactly."

"I once told you that you are undaunted, remember?"

"Yes, and I hadn't heard of that word before."

She smiles. "Trust me, it's true. You're undaunted, and you'll figure it out. I'm sure of it."

"Says you."

ENTER ROP
(REGIONAL OCCUPATIONAL PROGRAM)

Looking into the continuing education programs in our area, I discover the Regional Occupational Program (ROP), for adult learners. It meets at the Grossmont High School campus.

"Welcome, Mrs. Wagner. I've been expecting you."

My polyester pantsuit with the cloth flower on the jacket seems out of place as I look out over some fifteen or so high school seniors, finally spotting two men in their 40s and an elderly man, perhaps almost 60. The adults look up at me questioningly. Most of the high school students don't even look up, but the two that do have a certain look—doubt perhaps—that says, "She'll never last."

"I'm Mike, the instructor," says a middle-aged man with a broad smile. He looks like he might have been the football coach at one time. "Let me show you around. You can set down your briefcase in any one of the open stations."

I notice his desk in front of the classroom just to the right and decide to sit as close to it as possible, assuming I will have the most questions and need the most help.

"Are you an architect then, Mike?" I ask as I'm setting down my supplies.

"Well, no, not really, Mrs. Wagner."

"Oh please, just call me Janna."

"OK, Janna. No, I'm not exactly an architect. I've taught high school math here at Grossmont for fifteen years and was about to take early retirement when the principal asked me if I'd be able to teach a drafting class under the umbrella of ROP. He knew that while I was teaching math, I was also contracting, building, and selling homes on the side—one at a time, every two years or so. ROP sounded like an adventure, and I liked the idea of working with a variety of age groups, so I grabbed the opportunity, and here I am."

He explains that students can choose to use the old-fashioned vellum paper for renderings (drawings) or the new computer-assisted design program (CAD), which is all the rage at the moment, so it is in great demand by the high school-aged students.

"In fact," he says, "there are a limited number of CAD stations, but I'm willing to reserve one for you if you want the advantage of using it for your drawings. It's so much easier for most students to manage than the vellum."

"The vellum paper looks like a lot more fun to me," I say. "It's definitely prettier. I'll stay with the vellum. I've used it in my artwork from time to time. It comes in great big 28 × 34-inch sheets. Is that right?"

"Well, yes, that's true. But you might like to give the CAD program a try. Just let me know."

He's kind, and I can tell he wants me to try this new computer thing, but it's way out of my comfort zone.

Back to School, October 1987

With the kids settled into their classrooms, I start my drafting classes. I pick it up quickly and love penciling the image of what our add-on will look like onto vellum paper.

Since we've already gone *down* to gain space by digging out our basement, I figure we will go *up* in a cantilevered form above the kitchen, out over the lower terrace of the backyard. That will result in a three-story home with a great view as a bonus.

To me, the drawing looks quite lovely, functional, and certainly doable. The high school learners give me some weird sideways glances sometimes, but I don't let that discourage me. The oldsters in the class seem to enjoy using the *vellum process* as well. I have to hand it to the kids, though. Working with a computer seems to be second nature to them, and the 3D imaging is a nice feature.

Throughout the course, the instructor is very helpful. I am near the completion of my design. But before applying for permits for my design from the county, out of prudence I invite Mike to our home to look at the setting and to give me his final vote of confidence. After class, and with my plans in hand, we're off to our home for him to meet Larry and the kids and be impressed with my clever design.

Mike meets the family and is perfectly at peace with all the goings-on around him, even the high decibel level that is inevitable around that many kids. We look over the property together and finally sit down to go over the house plans and get the permit process organized.

As he sits down beside me at the far end of my drafting table, we spread out the vellum plans. I am brimming with enthusiasm and pride. After 15 minutes of quiet consideration, without eye contact, Mike rolls up my plans and hangs his head for a moment.

When he looks up, he says, "Janna, I know you're going to be disappointed, but this won't work for many reasons. First of all, this portion of the house you plan to stack onto is itself an old addition and not a sturdy one at that. You'd have to tear that down and start over from the ground up. That will add considerably to the cost of materials and labor, putting that option out of your reach."

I am crushed, my ambitions smashed. *How can this be? This is not what I had in mind at all!*

"Janna, you don't see it now, but your sons are going to grow up to be very big and will need a lot of room to run. Nothing you can do to your current home will effect an increase in the backyard large enough to accommodate four soon-to-be six-year-old boys. Blink your eyes and they'll be six feet tall."

Choking back tears, I raise my chin to look at him.

He goes on. "The lot you're living on now is steep. The terraces are not best for the kids in the long run. What you need to do is find an open lot for sale and build from the ground up, with a brand-new set of plans." He finishes with, "I know you're disappointed now, but I think you'll thank me later."

After Mike leaves, I throw myself on our bed, bury my head, and weep.

20

ROUND TWO

Ultimately, I am determined. I still hear Suzanne's words echoing in my head, "Janna, you are undaunted." *Now, how can I find an open lot at a reasonable price in San Diego County?*

The task begins with looking in the newspaper at the real estate listings for open lots.

Next, I'll need to drive all over the county, eyeballing lots, getting a feeling for the neighborhoods along the way. It reminds me of scouring the town in search of the perfect fabrics for a new quilting creation. It's basically shopping, and I'm good at that. *I'll make this into a fun adventure.*

Our main criterion is to find a lot in the neighborhood close to a community hub, with a school district that provides for *four* individual second-grade classrooms. The boys are currently in first grade, with two brothers in each room. The same setup we had for kindergarten, but with a different combination of brothers in each room. Finding a school with four second-grade classrooms will allow each of our sons to be the only Wagner in his room.

"OK, guys, ten more minutes before liftoff. Do you have all your gear?" The Thursday 7:45 a.m. morning countdown has begun. As I apply the finishing touches of makeup, I check the mirror in our small bathroom, then step out to be sure my black pantsuit with the white collared shirt looks sharp enough to go lot shopping.

Kyle sprints out to the front porch with his lunch pail, completed assignments, and his jacket in hand, ready to go. He has morphed into a six-year-old who doesn't know what it means to walk. Wherever he is going, it's always at a dead run. A fleeting flashback reminds me of his first year and a half, moving as slow as a sloth.

Back then, Gramma Norma commented that I shouldn't worry. "He just doesn't want to waste energy, Janna. He's deep in thought. He wants to invest his energy watching the other guys work things out before he decides to make his moves."

Maybe she had it right.

This morning, he bypasses the traditional calling out of "Shotgun" altogether. He is settled in the van, seat belt latched, before his brothers are even headed down the steps.

"OK, guys, just five minutes left. Get a move on. Remember, you get a sticker if you're ready to go before Mommy gets in the driver's seat."

Adjusting the mirrors, I say, "Looks like Daddy's coming down to say goodbye. Get ready for hugs and tickles."

"Hey, Daddy, what are you doing today?" Ben asks.

"I'm going to train a new teacher at the music school today."

"Is she a nice lady?" Brett asks.

"Actually, Brett, this teacher is a man."

"Does he play piano good?" Chad asks.

"Yes, Chad, he plays very well, and I hope he'll be a really good teacher."

"Mommy, you look pretty," Ben says. "Are you shopping for a lot today?"

"Yep, I sure am."

"Did you find one yet?"

"No, not yet. I've been shopping every day for three weeks. I still haven't found the right lot. I think we're going to need to pray for a miracle."

"Everybody bow your head. I'm going to pray for Mommy," Ben orders.

"Hey, Ben," Larry says. "Maybe you can say your prayer when Mommy is driving. It's time for her to go now."

"Yeah, my teacher gets really mad if I'm not in my seat at the right time," Kyle says.

A Troubling Snag

After school, when I pull into the school to pick up the kids, a shock is in store for me.

This day seems like any other until I reach the second classroom. I hug Chad, help him gather his gear, and then walk over to hug Kyle to help him get his stuff together as well. Kyle has long blond bangs and it looks like he has a little dirt underneath his cute little hairs. I lift his bangs to clean him up when I am stunned and furious to see, written in capital letters with a black marker across his forehead, "LISTEN!" I contain myself for his benefit. I calmly ask him, "Who wrote this?"

"My teacher," he says.

Hugging him again, I choke back my tears and fury, gather my other two sons, and walk them all out to the exit, requesting that one of the other teachers ask the principal to come over for a moment—that I have something for her.

When she arrives, I look her in the eye and say, "This is just between you and me right now, but I want you to see something." With the other kids going ahead so that they won't see, I raise Kyle's bangs, look her in the eye, and say, "I will call you when I get home."

At home, I take a picture, then clean off his forehead. The boys get busy with their snacks and I find a private place to make my call.

The teacher is older, perhaps a senior citizen. Maybe she has just lost her patience with teaching altogether. But, that's no excuse for losing control in such a way that she felt writing that message on a child's forehead was OK. Did she think it wasn't even wrong? Witness the fact that she didn't even think to at least erase the evidence from Kyle's forehead before mama bear arrived to take him home. What does that tell me about her perspective on things? I just can't fathom it.

As soon as my boys are playing happily in the backyard, I say a prayer, take a deep breath, and initiate my call to the principal.

After a short round of hellos, we get to it. "Mrs. Wagner," the principal begins, "I can only imagine how distressing this must be for you. I assure you that I will remedy the situation and that there will be severe repercussions for the teacher. I am so sorry for what you and your family must be going through."

Together, Larry and I decide that for the benefit of Kyle and our entire family, we should not make a public issue of it.

The next morning, as my friend Susie greets me in the parking lot of the school, it takes every ounce of restraint I can muster to keep it to myself. I so want to talk to her about it. But life is long, word gets around, and you can't take words back once they've been said.

"Hey, Janna, are you there?" Susie asks. "You seem like you're off in another world."

"No, I'm here," I say. "How are you?"

"Oh, I'm great. I got a call last night that they were going to be moving some of the teachers around today."

"Oh, really?"

"Yeah. Jonathan really likes the teacher that's coming to his classroom. She taught one of the intersession classes in the summer—he loved it."

Sure enough, after Brett and Ben walk to their classroom on their own, I walk Chad and Kyle to theirs to discover that they have a new teacher as well. *That puts out the fire for now.*

I learn later from the principal that Kyle's teacher has been sent to a different school to teach. That is completely incomprehensible to me. It seems like it should have been grounds for a complete dismissal from the school system, at the very least. But, again, for my own children's benefit, I choose not to make a scene about it. Our family has been in local and national news many times, and any controversy we might engage in would certainly be of public interest. I imagine what it might be like for Kyle and our family to be in the public eye for something like this. So, for many years I pray for the well-being of any children put in her care and for insight on her part. I pray that she will be remorseful, but I realize that to contact us with an apology would be an admission of wrongdoing, and that is something she probably feels she can't risk.

A legal three-ring circus in the public eye would be of no benefit to our son, after the fact. So, we go on with our lives, with me more determined than ever to solve our housing challenge and move on.

DEAD ENDS END—MAY 1988

After many days of dead ends, I turn the corner to go up to the community of Jamul for a look-see. Jamul is in the rural southeast area of San Diego County. My homework the night before informed me that the lots have a one-acre minimum requirement, the soil is mostly decomposed granite, and that there are no sewers.

I'd seen an advertisement about a community with a total of six empty lots, with only one still available for purchase. I fall in love with it the moment I open the van door and step out, filling my lungs with sweet, fresh, country air. As I walk the perimeter of the lot, I notice a creek bed with lots of native plants, including native manzanita bushes. On the other side of the creek is a cistern, with water in it. It also has a great view of the rolling hills and has what I think would be added value. The lot backs up to a 35-acre parcel of empty land, also full of native plants. That might mean our kids could have access to that 35 acres to explore. The price is just about within our reach. However, the population density of Jamul is very sparse, and it seems highly unlikely that there will be four separate second-grade classrooms at the local school, which is the litmus test for me.

◆　　◆　　◆　　◆

The school secretary makes an appointment for me at 10:00 a.m. with the principal, Diana Damschen. *What a warm, inviting demeanor she has*, I think, as she walks into the waiting room to greet me.

"You must be Mrs. Wagner," she says, as she reaches out her hand and gives me a firm handshake. "I'm so glad that you've come here to look at our school district."

"Well, I have to be honest. I really don't know much about the school district, as I've never visited before."

Without hesitation she waves her arm, inviting me to join her on a tour of the elementary school. I am taken by how warm, outgoing, and relaxed she is.

"I should tell you before we even get started that we have four seven-year-old sons that I need to place in second-grade classrooms."

She almost seems to miss a step as she pauses in her stride and turns to look directly at me. "Did you say four sons, all the same age?"

I nod, observing her reaction to the news, thinking it might be too much for a small rural school.

"Well, that's wonderful. You must be so proud. I certainly hope we can work things out so that your sons can attend Jamul Elementary School this fall."

Well, that's one hurdle. She asks me more about what brings me here to the Jamul-Dulzura School District.

"Do you have an extended family in the neighborhood or a close friend?"

"Not in Jamul."

"You will find that people are very friendly here, and we will do all we can to make you feel welcome and comfortable."

"That's very generous of you," I say, not mentioning that we don't yet have a home in this school district. "There is one hurdle that we need to jump in order to go further. I'm guessing your answer will be no."

"Try me, and we'll see if we can work it out."

"We have our mind set on placing our sons in a school where each boy can be in a classroom without any of his brothers," I say. "Wait. … What I mean is, we want each of them to be seen as individuals and we want to do all we can to accommodate that goal. So, we have our minds set on enrolling them in a school that has four individual second-grade classrooms."

"I can definitely understand your desire to be in that kind of setting," she says.

As I prepare my mind and heart for a letdown, she continues. "I can assure you we do have four second-grade classes on the schedule for this fall, and we would be delighted to enroll each of your children in one of them."

What I really want to do is turn toward her and give her a big bear hug. Control yourself, Janna. "Well then, I'd better jump to it and put in an offer right away for the lot we have in mind. I'll get back to you just as quickly as I can, but I can't help but think that this is meant to be."

"I certainly hope so," she says.

◆　◆　◆　◆

Arriving with the whole family to check out the lot, Larry isn't quite as excited about it as I hoped he would be. *But hey, he just doesn't have that quilty thing going on. He just needs more time to warm up to the idea. True, the lot has a hundred-year flood plain, which limits the buildable portion considerably. But it seems like the 35 acres of open space behind us, coupled with the indigenous plants, and 1.3 acres of land that will be ours, more than offsets those limitations in value.*

The kids nearly trample each other climbing out of the van and running to all the nine red-flagged corners of the lot. Within twenty minutes they are all covered with dirt after running through all the bushy trails and gathering as many boulders as possible to begin making a fortress of protection for what they assume will be our future home. No one mentioned that there might be poison oak in the area.

21

ROUND THREE—IF THEN

As I walk back into the ROP class, Mike looks up. "Hi, Coach Mike. I'm ready to learn how to design a home from the ground up."

He opens his mouth to say something.

I interrupt before he gets started. "I enrolled in this class to learn how to make house plans. We found a lot we want to build on. We've put in an offer. I'd like to start on the plans even before we get the go-ahead from the bank."

There is a pause. "I'll help you get started," he says. "Just realize you might have to face some disappointments if things don't go through."

"I'm willing to take the chance."

◆　◆　◆　◆

The plans get done quickly. All we need now is a bunch of money. *That's what savings and loan companies are all about, right?* One thing is in our favor: our friend Rick, who helped us build under our current house, has agreed that if we get the construction loan, he will do the work as our contractor.

God, please open doors that might otherwise close in our faces. Or, if this door should remain shut, we will trust you for the outcome of that as well.

With the whole family strapped in, we're off to the savings and loan in La Mesa.

Larry and the boys get settled in the lobby. I am to be the spokesperson.

Turning to walk up the steps to meet the loan officer, I whisper, "Pray for me, guys."

As planned, I open with greetings and statements of respect and awe at the creativity and skill the bank has in financial dealings—how I have admired their bank for years as a pillar of the community. The lady, well dressed and articulate, is very professional. *I'll have to appeal to her big heart and motherly instincts,* I decide. Next, I segue into asking, "Do you happen to remember those quadruplets born to a La Mesa couple about seven years ago?"

She nods. "Yes. It was all over the news."

"Well, that's us! Here are some then-and-now snapshots of the boys." I pause as she looks through the photos, then continue, "And we need to give those four boys a bit more space to grow."

Taking a deep breath to still my heart, I lead off with the phrase that I've been practicing for the past two days.

"We want to offer you the first opportunity to be the lender who makes it a possibility."

Looking over the pictures, she asks, "Oh my, how do you ever manage four at once? They look so happy and fit."

Shifting back into business mode, she says, "Let's look at your contractor's qualifications, your background, your credit rating, and any collateral. I'm sure we can work something out."

She views the papers showing the contractor, the house plans, some equity in our current home, some eleven years of owning our music school—and at my charming, convincing smiles. That, coupled with her La Mesa pride, tender heart, and our "think outside the box" strategies bring us to a viable solution. In the end, the bank agrees to grant us a construction loan, which will pay for the lot and all building costs. They will hold a lien against our La Mesa home as collateral. Without receiving any money down from us, the bank takes an unprecedented risk on us, but we won't break their trust and it could turn out to be mutually beneficial not just in the loan value but as publicity for them.

Permit Path

"Larry, this is so much more than I bargained for."

"Well, isn't that just about the way life goes? Hasn't every project we've ever done been more than we bargained for after all is said and done?"

"Yeah, that's right, but I wouldn't mind if there was an exception to that rule now and then."

"Want to tell me all about it?"

"Yes," I nod.

"How 'bout after the kids get in bed. Can you wait that long?"

"Do I have my choice?"

"All right then, after dinner it is."

Later on, I start with, "So, are you OK with being in listening mode while I dump all this worrisome stuff on you?"

"I don't mind listening, as long as you're gonna find your answers to your problems by contacting Mike in ROP, someone who really knows what he's doing."

"It's a deal. Here goes …"

I begin to list for Larry the endless volume of requirements and hoops to jump through just to get permits.

Halfway through the list, Larry says, "Whew, I'm just glad you're the mathy one."

"Not mathy enough, methinks. I may have to default to the *fake it until you make it* routine somewhere along the line."

Before submitting the plans to the county, I have them engineered by a professional. Next, I gather up the first series of plans to be approved by the county and begin the process of patiently (or not so patiently) waiting in the county office for my turn. I am told to just submit them and go home—but I am impatient. So, I bake banana bread for the inspectors, to bring along with the plans, and I am sure to have a good book to read for any wait time. Whenever I get a chance to confer with the county agent regarding our permits, I come in with a loaf of banana bread and a smile, hoping for the best. I'm sure it's the banana bread working its charm, as things seem to be going very smoothly.

A WELCOME CALL

One day, the phone rings. "Hello," I say with bated breath.

The man on the other end of the line says, "Your permits have been approved. You can come in and get your stamped building plans and begin your project."

Larry is ready to head for his afternoon music classes for the day. I am about to explode with excitement. But I tell myself, I've waited far too long for this day to be in a hurry about it now.

Biting my tongue to control my excitement, I calmly tell the kids to stop their gymnastics and come sit in the living room for a huddle. They've been feisty with each other this morning, and several time-outs have been assigned throughout the day. A glance at their expressions makes it clear that each of them thinks that Mom is controlling herself just long enough to let them know how much trouble they are in.

"Ben, go get Daddy from my office at the top of the hill."

"Okay, Mommy."

"Go quickly now, but be careful not to stumble. Daddy is probably just finishing his lesson plans, so he might be a little bit impatient about being interrupted. Don't worry, he's not mad at you."

"Are you mad at me, Mommy?"

"Not at all, Ben. You just go get Daddy."

Five minutes later, Larry bolts in the door with Ben close behind.

"Is everything OK, honey?" he asks as he walks into the living room with Ben.

"Yes, everything is going to be fine, but …" I pause for effect. "Well, you see, the thing is …" I look down at the floor and turn to glance at each one of them.

"Is it your parents … are they OK?" Larry asks, concerned.

Realizing I am taking this a little bit too far, I look up, give a smile to each one individually, finishing with Larry at the end of the line and shout, "I just got a call from the county, and our permits have been approved. We can start building our house now."

The whole room bursts into screaming and shouts of joy.

"Tomorrow after school when Daddy is at work, we'll take a field trip to pick up our permits."

◆ ◆ ◆ ◆

Heavy traffic on the freeway to downtown or not, I load my guys into the van and we all go to the county building permit office.

"When we walk into the permit office, you will be very good boys," I say. "You will keep your hands in your pockets, no touching a brother, not even with your elbow, and you will smile at the people in the office. The people in the county building will be so amazed at how well-behaved you guys are. It will make all of them smile big. You will be the best-behaved seven-year-old boys they've ever seen. But most importantly, when we get home, I'll be able to tell Daddy just how proud I am of you."

We get more than a couple of looks as we walk down the hallway with the kids, single file behind me, all with their hands in their pockets.

◆ ◆ ◆ ◆

Within a week, we secure a contract with Dixieline Lumber to carry our account and deliver the building materials to our Jamul lot as needed per the construction loan parameters.

Plans are made for the kids to attend Jamul Elementary for the next school year, each in their own second-grade classroom. Meanwhile, they're finishing up their current year-round session.

"Mommy, where are we going to live while we're building the house," Chad asks. "Are we going to get a trailer to live in?"

"That's a really good idea, Chad," I say.

"So, we get to live in a big long trailer?" He looks at me hopefully.

"Well, honey, I really wish we could, but they have some rules about not having a trailer on the lot."

"Why?"

"Well, it's complicated, but it's just a rule they have, and we have to keep that rule."

"But you said that you will be at the lot each day when they're working."

"Yes, that's true."

"But where will you live? Will you have to sleep in your car at night?"

"OK, Chad, I think it's time for another huddle. Let's get everyone together. Can you round up your brothers in the living room for me?"

"OK. I'll be right back."

"Thanks, Chad. I love you."

"I love you too, Mommy."

"Everybody settled now?" I ask. "Who is confused about where you're going to live and how we will do this building-a-house thing?" All hands go up. "OK, Daddy and I have a plan. It will be a great adventure for you. Mommy or Daddy will drop you off at school in the usual place, just like we do now. Then, Daddy will do music schoolwork, and Mommy will take some banana bread up to the workers at our lot in Jamul. I will stay there in case they have any questions or need me to run and get something for them or need me to clean up the building site. Mostly, we just think they might do their best work if somebody is there to cheer them on. That's me. I'm going to clean up and cheer them on."

"But, Mommy," Kyle says, "you clean at home. Do you have to clean up the lot too?"

"Somebody told me that construction workers are sometimes really messy, and they don't always clean up after themselves. The workers have all told us that they would give us a really good deal on the price of building the house, so I figure that means I might have to do the cleaning up for them."

"OK," Kyle says.

"So, when you are done with school for the day, Mommy or Daddy will pick you up."

"Will we ever get to live at the lot?" Brett asks.

"Yes, but not until the house is all made. It takes time to build a house. So, we have to be patient. While the house is being built, we will still live here in La Mesa."

"When do we get to go to our new classrooms in Jamul?" Brett asks.

"You just have a few weeks before your school finishes up here in La Mesa. Then in September, you'll get to go to school in Jamul with your new friends."

"Do we do our homework at our house or at the lot?" Brett asks.

"We will have to work that out as we go. Until the house is finished, we will all sleep here, in the same house with Mommy and Daddy, no matter what."

◆　◆　◆　◆

I begin my daily habit of going up to the lot to play the role of owner-contractor and pretend I know what I'm doing. All the time I am depending on the grace of God, the trustworthiness of the subcontractors, and the power of freshly baked bread to fill the gaps in my construction acumen.

I need to keep a predictable routine going for everyone's benefit. But I don't know if that's possible.

22

DIRT, WATER, AND TRACTORS

"Oh man, Larry. I'm not sure I realized what I was getting myself into."

"How so?"

"Well, for starters, Chuck was going over how the grading plan works. We met at the lot because he wanted to be sure I understand the process of attaching the fire hose to the fire hydrant at the corner of our lot."

"He wants to have you do that?" he asks, with raised eyebrows and surprise.

"No, he just wants me to understand the process. He said that unless we get some rain between now and Monday, the DG ..."

"DG?"

"Decomposed granite. Without rain, the DG will remain as hard as concrete, and the dirt won't be soft enough to grade— you know, to sculpt it into the shape we want it to be."

"So, what do we do about that?"

"That's where the fire hose comes into play. He explained to me that he would be spending hours holding and controlling the fire hose as it blows out a fan of water some 75 to 100 feet across our property."

"Wow, that's impressive."

"Yeah, that's the truth. Anyway, he says after that, the dirt will be soft enough to grade. But it might take a few days for the DG to soften enough for them to actually start grading. I just put on my confident 'I understand this stuff' look as he went on."

"Is there more?"

"Oh yeah—then he started throwing in words like GPM (gallons per minute) and PSI (pounds per square inch)."

"And you comprehended all that?"

"Not on your life. I was writing notes on my clipboard like crazy."

"Oh, baby, come to Papa. You must have been so freaked out."

I collapse into his hug. "Oh, honey, thank you so much for understanding. I'm so glad that you're not laughing at me." I begin to laugh a little bit at myself.

"So, what did you do?"

"Well, for one thing, I was very grateful that we were having this conversation on Thursday, and he won't be doing that fire hose thing until Monday. So, I poked around a little bit and made some calls to the fire station, since we'd have to use their fire hydrant."

"The fire station? You're kidding."

"Nah, I figure when they're not busy fighting fires and such, they maybe get bored and might welcome the chance to answer some questions about their job and what it's like to be a fireman."

"That's my girl."

"Did you know that PSI varies considerably from area to area? And Oscar, my new fireman friend, said that it even varies by the various neighborhood activities going on at any given time."

"Makes sense."

"Yep, and I know you're half teasing me for being so excited about this. But I think it's really pretty interesting—like the water pressure can be lower in the morning hours when many residents are taking showers, or when there's a big fire to put out, or there's a big building project going on that relies on water pressure. He said that in Jamul, graders pretty much need the hose before and during the whole excavating process. Anyway, I think our guys will go wild with excitement over all that water flying across the lot, don't you think?"

"No doubt. But remember, honey, the plans were engineered by a pro, and all the subcontractors are pros at their jobs. You don't have to completely understand everything that's being done at the property. You just have to be sure that each job gets done in a timely fashion, right?"

"Yep, I guess you're right, but I'm still pretty nervous about the grading."

"Well, I plan to be there when the grading gets started too. You can lean on me. Would that be good?"

"Oh, man, that would be wonderful."

"I know the boys will have fun with this process. I think you and I will have fun too!"

What seven-year-old boy doesn't enjoy playing in the dirt, riding on tractors, and exploring the countryside? On these hot summer days in Jamul, before school starts, they'll get to share the excitement of seeing a grading dozer up close as the grading is done on the lot.

The marvel of watching the operator drive his machine with fast and skilled accuracy gets their imaginations going, and they come up with all sorts of plans for what they will do and what they will build once we settle into our new neighborhood.

THE GRADING PROCESS

Our lot is steep. The 100-year floodplain means we can't build in the area that floods, which it does, on average, once each century. Paired with the designated area for leach lines, it makes for a relatively small building area, even though the total size of the lot is one-and-a-third acres.

"Janna, we'll have to do a cut-and-fill process to create a pad for your house," Chuck tells me as he is about finished with the initial grading.

"Tell me about it," I ask authoritatively.

"Basically, with cut and fill, the amount of material from the cut portion of dirt roughly matches the amount of fill needed for nearby embankments. The goal is to get the pad to the exact height shown in the plans."

"Makes sense so far."

"After the cut is made, the fill has to be well compacted, so that it will be stable."

"I see." This is *project-based learning* in its purest form.

"To do that, we'll still be using the grading dozer. You might want to leave your kids home for that. These machines can be dangerous—lethal."

"Thanks for the warning."

Larry and I are at the lot to watch the drama after dropping the kids at school. When Larry has to leave for the music school, I head back to La Mesa, pick up the kids, and bring them to the lot in Jamul. *I hope I won't regret this.*

The fire hose is attached to the fire hydrant and the men begin spraying. After many serious warnings of possible danger, we all get out of the van to watch the show. Taking Chuck's warning seriously, I walk the kids twenty yards out from our red-flagged lot borderline, then up the steep hill toward the huge bolder that marks the end of our lot.

It's muddy and slippery. We are just about at the top when I see Kyle look out over his left shoulder as some sprinkles fall on him. His footing doesn't quite look secure. I push myself up and reach to secure my right arm so I can give him a push up with my left arm. Grabbing onto a root with my right hand, I push him up with my left. But the root is not secure and comes right out of the dirt. Slipping down about two feet I grab another root, which holds.

"Mommy, are you okay?" Kyle yells.

"Yes, I'm OK. Just a little embarrassed, and a lot dirty."

"You have to be careful, Mommy," Chad says. "Do you want me to pull you up?"

"Thanks, Chad. I'm OK. I think that was meant to be a wake-up call."

After a second round of grading with the fabulous fire hose and lots of water, I end up with four mud-encrusted seven-year-old boys, no injuries, and with all limbs intact.

A FIRM FOUNDATION

I am insisting on an unorthodox foundation for our home. It has solid logic behind it, even if the engineer says he hasn't seen this kind of design before. I can't see building a home with interior walls that stay static, year after year. What if I change my mind somewhere along the line? I want to be able to move an interior wall without it being a big deal. Because the house will be two stories, an unfinished basement storage area below and a living area on top, we might even want to put some new walls in the lower-level basement someday. I used to know very little about walls until I took that drafting class— learning where walls go and how they stay stable. I now know that conducting the weight of the upper-level solid foundation is key. I think of it as displacing the weight to the outside, a little easier for my mind to grasp. Thanks to Mike, now I get it. Well, sort of, anyway.

The whole house and foundation will be built on a cutout portion of the sloping hillside. There will be stem walls on both sides and a retaining wall at the back to secure the foundation and guarantee that water won't leak from the hill behind.

"You know what, Larry? I never want to forget how impressed and grateful I feel right now for the engineer and all the skilled people that are making this house a possibility."

"Ditto," Larry says. "I'd better scoot over to the music school if I want to get back by 2:45."

◆　◆　◆　◆

I see Larry driving down the street at 2:45 exactly, right on time to pick up the kids.

"How did your teacher training and demo lesson go? Did you hook a few?" I ask as we both get into the van to pick up the guys at school.

"I think this new teacher is a keeper."

"Wow, things just keep getting better, don't they?"

"How do you think the kids did at school today?" Larry asks.

"We shall see."

◆　◆　◆　◆

Picking them up from school at the end of the day leaves no doubt that we made the right choice. The family interaction as they talk about their individual experiences is *off the charts.*

Larry heads back to the music school. I head over to the lot with the boys to spend the afternoon, where they will run off some energy for a while, playing in the dirt and hiking in the creek bed.

I spread out a big blanket, set out four clipboards, some paper, four pencils, and their assignments.

"Here's how we'll do this, guys. You'll use your clipboards to do your schoolwork and I'll be here to help you. We'll stay out of the way of the workers so they can get their job done."

They settle down to do their schoolwork as I bask in the joy of watching each of them fill out the heading with their name and their own individual teacher's name. Each son seems to think his teacher is great. *They are not doing much comparing—not what I was expecting. What a relief that they aren't wrapped up in an argument about whose teacher or class is best. Each boy seems to already have a loyalty to his own teacher.*

My hope for this family is being fulfilled. I'll probably look back on this time and say, "These are some of the happiest days of my life." I'm seeing the dream of having our own custom home develop in front of my eyes, while at the same time our children are growing into their custom selves. Not one of them is just like any of his brothers. For that matter, not one of them is like any other person on this planet.

I wonder if any of them will ever look back on this day and realize what a difference it made in his life.

23

MOVIN' ON UP

"Hey, guys, we did it," I announce.

"Did it?" Ben asks.

"First of all, you've chosen all the gifts from Mommy's secret store that you'll give to each other for Christmas, right?"

They all nod.

"And there is something even more exciting. Go get your jammies, toothbrushes, and a change of clothes. It's a surprise. Dad is up at our Jamul house with an ice chest and our camping gear."

Chad looks at me. "Do we get to sleep there tonight?"

"Yep, we're going to have a Christmas Eve sleepover at our new home."

As soon as the yelling, cheering, hugging, and high fives die down a bit, they start throwing their gear in their backpacks.

The boys think it's just a one-night sleepover. What they don't know is that it's actually the first step of the long-awaited move-in. Against all odds, we achieve our goal and move in on Christmas Eve. As Dad turns up the volume on the cassette player, Cool and the Gang sing "Celebration," and we dance like maniacs on the plywood floors—even Dad.

◆　◆　◆　◆

On Christmas morning, with Dad and the boys still asleep, I grab a cup of coffee and walk out on the deck. Opening the sliding door, the sharp, sweet, refreshing smell of pine trees engulfs me. A coyote begins to howl, soon joined by two more. As the howling dies down, it strikes me that we are entering a whole new era. Though we are a mere four miles from the essentials, the country has a distinct ambiance of its own.

Scanning my new surroundings, I marvel at how my modest architectural plans have come to fruition. The cantilevered first floor has 1800 square feet of floor space. Our wraparound deck, which looks out to the mountains across the valley, adds another 600 square feet.

It's San Diego County, with an average temperature of 70 degrees. I bet the kids will spend as much time running around on this deck and in the yard as they do in the house. That's what I'll be shooting for anyway.

We'll develop the downstairs unfinished basement area eventually. For now, it can be used for storage. *No doubt the kids will spend most of their time outside anyway.*

"Mom … Mom," I hear Brett say, as he opens the sliding door. "Can we wake up Dad now?"

"Yes, go for it."

"Come on, guys, we get to wake up Dad."

The boys run into the master bedroom where Dad is curled up in our double sleeping bag. It's a dogpile. I lean against the door frame appreciating the scene as I mark it in my memory.

"OK, guys, time to let Daddy get up and get his coffee."

Winking at Larry, I announce to the boys, "It looks like you have something in your stockings."

They all scramble to be the first ones to the fireplace. Kyle gets there first and runs with his stocking into our new dining room, stuffing marshmallow Santas into his mouth along the way. Chad, Ben, and Brett join in, as they all start dumping out the contents onto the table, checking to be sure everything is fair and square and that no one has more goodies than anyone else.

"Look, Mom. Look what's in our yard," Kyle gawks.

"Oh my, look at that."

"What is it?" Brett, Chad, and Ben ask at once.

"Oh man," Chad says. "Is that a good thing, Mommy?"

"Not so much. Maybe you'd better go get Daddy."

Larry is already on his way to the dining room when all the boys point out through the window toward the huge lawn area. "It seems we have some uninvited visitors this morning."

"Oh, !#@!" Larry exclaims.

Everybody points and begins to count. We seem to have the happiest bunnies in Jamul—35 of them, to be exact—all feasting on our newly laid sod. *My brain is short-circuiting on this one. How did we not see this coming?*

OUR NEW LIFE

"Remember talking about how short the ride would be to the school once we moved into our new house?" I ask. "That day is here. Grab your stuff, get in the van, and let's do this. I bet it won't take more than five minutes to get to school."

We all wanted to move in at Christmas, whether the tile and carpet were laid or not.

"I'll lay tile while you're at the office and the kids are at school," I tell Larry. "If it takes more time than that, I can just do a couple of hours in the evening when they're in bed. Shouldn't be a problem."

After the first few days, I get into the rhythm of that promise. After the boys are tucked in for the night, I set the tile, beginning with the hallways. For protection, I cover it with a strip of plywood afterward so it can be walked on as it sets. During the day when the guys are at school, I fill in the grout lines.

I have run into a couple of snags: (1) There's the hauling of five-gallon buckets of water back and forth to deal with, and (2) it is difficult to make the grout lines level. Since I don't mind getting messy and dirty, I opt to speed up and improve the process by getting rid of my gloves. I like the feeling of pushing the grout into the grooves with my fingertips. I soon discover that there is lye in the grout, and it burns like acid. Now, I've got little holes in my fingers that leave an unrelenting caustic sting. It seems to be eating away the skin at my fingertips.

I recall that Mom had told me more than once, "Jan, you be anything you want to be."

Today I discovered that I don't want to be a tiler.

◆　◆　◆　◆

The surrounding lots in the neighborhood are beginning to take shape as other homeowners begin to build. Our foursome has grown to a group of six boys who all play in the creek bed, on the lawn, and down the street. Two of our new neighbors have kids about the same age named Cailin and Anthony. Those families are almost finished building and are close to moving in. Up to this point, it has been quite idyllic here at our new spread … until today. It's Saturday morning, and Chad comes into our room bright and early.

In a fairly loud whisper, he asks, "Mom, are you awake?"

"I am now."

"Can I go outside to play?"

"It's only 6:30, Chad."

"But I have a cool plan and I want to go outside and build something."

"Hold on. I'll come out, but let's not wake up Daddy."

Turns out he wants to build a fort. There are no other occupied houses around yet, so I figure it won't interrupt anybody's sleep, so why not?

"Can I use your drafting cubby in the sewing closet?" he asks. "I wanna make a plan."

"Sure, good idea."

As he munches down his Golden Grahams cereal, he sketches his vision.

I'm sipping my coffee as I watch. Within a few minutes, he finishes with a determined look on his face. As he proceeds to gather scrap wood from our various building projects, he asks to use one of our leather toolbelts.

Then he heads to the garage to gather some basic tools—hammer, saw, level, some leather gloves, a T-bar for good measure, and of course a helmet. After gathering a variety of nails, screws, and a screwdriver, he is on the way to the end of the lawn near the creek bed.

"Careful there, son. That's a bit of a steep area you're headed for."

"I'm gonna make a treehouse."

"Just watch your footing."

"I will," he says, as he turns and starts running toward the creek bed, his oversized tool belt flapping up and down against his slim hips.

Larry wakes up, grabs a cup of coffee, and joins me. We watch Chad from the dining room window, still in our jams. All is well. His brothers are sleeping right through any noise he makes during his 7:00 a.m. project.

He quickly runs out of wood scraps. Heading up to the garage, he grabs some heavy-duty insulated Romex wire, leftovers from the electrical jobs.

Back in the house with Larry, watching this busy bee work it, I ask, "What's he gonna do with that, I wonder?"

"I'm guessing he won't be running electrical, but I'll keep a close watch," Larry replies. "Don't worry, there's no electricity down there and he doesn't have any electrical tools with him.

"I see what he's doing," Larry says. "He's running the Romex horizontally back and forth, dodging the manzanita branches ... probably trying to create some sort of level platform. Clever."

Part of the beauty of our place is the wild manzanita bushes, with beautiful red bark and branches that twist around in varied directions, each one creating its own original design. They are an endangered species, so can't be removed from the lot.

Chad looks like he's getting a bit frustrated with all of the beautiful branches of the tree he is trying to build his fort in. He takes the liberty of breaking the tops off some of the branches and throwing them to the side to deal with later. All of a sudden, he loses his footing and slips off the large branch he is standing on, falling between the Romex wires. On the way down, he lands on a sharp manzanita root protruding from the ground. He reaches out to grab onto a nearby branch, screaming in agony.

"Chad! Don't move, I'm coming," Larry yells, running at top speed.

I quickly wake up Ben, Brett, and Kyle. "Wake up, wake up. Take a pee and get right into the van, no questions asked," I bellow.

"What's wrong, Mommy? Where is Chad?" Ben demands.

"Chad's hurt, but he's going to be just fine. No more questions."

Having had some first-aid training, I know it's sometimes best to leave a puncture wound alone—best to leave it to the physician's judgment. Poor Chad is miserable as we drive, leaning to one side with his seatbelt around him, so as not to put any pressure on the puncture wound.

Thankfully, all goes well, and there is no damage to any tissues that need stitching. They give Chad antibiotics and patch him up with some tight bandages.

SETTLING IN

"Which doorway do I sit in tonight, Jan?" Larry asks.

"Do you remember who you sat across from last night?"

"I think I was across from Chad and Brett, and you were across from Ben and Kyle. Does that sound right?"

"Yeah, I think that's right."

"OK, so let's switch."

"I've got it, and I've got the book as well," I say.

I recall how excited I was when I went to Barnes and Noble to look for a book that we could read together to our kids every evening before bed. The one with the drawing of four little boys gathered together by their mom and dad grabbed my interest. *Little Visits with God* looked like it might be good, I remember thinking. As I skimmed through it, I was impressed that each short bedtime story was a lesson in character building, followed by a short paragraph that brought the message home, called "Let's Talk About This." I bought it as a Christmas gift that we could start using when we moved in. What a find.

With both of us sitting on the hallway floor, facing their open bedroom doors, they climb into their bunk beds and Larry begins to read.

"OK, this story is called, 'How to Keep from Doing Wrong.'"

As Larry reads, I have the luxury of watching our kids and enjoying their expressions. The story is about two kids who just can't resist picking the ripe berries from their neighbors' yard without asking. As the story unfolds, Ben seems to be getting restless. Nothing surprising for a seven-year-old boy. But, when we are just about to start the "Let's Talk About This" section, he begins to tear up, squirming a little more than usual. "Are you OK, honey? Do you need a hug?" I ask.

Ben takes a deep breath and begins to unload.

"Remember the dirt and matches thing we got caught doing right after we moved in?" Ben begins.

Just as I began to respond, Kyle yells, "I didn't do that, Mommy. It was just Ben and Brett and Chad."

"Yes, Kyle, I know it wasn't you. Now let Ben talk. Go ahead, Ben."

"Right after we moved in, all of us but Kyle got caught trying to make dirt bombs at the bottom of Anthony's property. We used two-liter soda bottles filled with dirt and a piece of twine as a fuse."

"Yes, I remember that."

"We got caught one by one by his mom when we went up to check for more matches in their garage, and she was standing there. I was last because I went up to see why no one came back. She sent us all down with a little head start to confess to you guys. She said she'd call to be sure that we had told you."

"Yes, I remember that phone call."

"In fact," Larry says, "we restricted all of you to your rooms for a week."

"What else, Ben?" I ask.

"You took us to the fire station to watch an arson video."

"Yes, Ben. And you've been forgiven, remember?"

"But, Mommy, I need to tell you one more thing."

"What's that?"

"It was my idea," he says, hanging his head.

Larry and I look at each other. "We didn't know that," I say. "Would you feel better if we prayed again about it?"

"Yes, Mommy. I'd like that."

"You don't need me to say the prayer, son. You can just talk to God yourself, out loud if you want. He's just like a friend that's by you all the time, and he loves to forgive you when you mess up."

"Thanks, Mommy."

◆　◆　◆　◆

The nighttime tiling episodes are getting extremely old. The hallway is finished and the dining room is well on its way with pavers. But I'm caving in and hiring someone to finish the job.

The person I hire is very good at what she does. She makes it look easy. As she sets the tile, her son and our boys play together. She is smart enough to wear gloves, and her hands have no holes in them like mine. *I wonder how long it will take for my hands to regain their youthful beauty, if ever.*

Today marks a week that she's been tiling, but now it's finally finished. I realize that sometimes it's just not worth doing everything yourself. Besides, it puts someone else to work, someone who is experienced and who has their own tools.

With the tiling job completed, the piano is moved into the dining room, and the daily practice routine gets in gear again.

24

LOAN CONVERSION

The next step in this whole home-building adventure is to convert our construction loan to a conventional thirty-year mortgage and sell our La Mesa home.

Sitting at the breakfast table, Larry brings up the subject. "This could be some pretty tricky timing," he says.

"Tell me about it. I don't know how this whole thing is supposed to work. Do you?"

"Well, the building cost and the property itself comes to $168,000."

"Larry, that's such a great deal."

"And you know, Jan, you were so right when you said we'd get more land and house for our money as owner-builders."

"It really helped that the subs gave us good deals too. Still, we are staring at a boatload of debt."

Looking over the paperwork, Larry pauses. "It should be no problem to get a mortgage, and the payments should be low. The challenge will be making payments on the La Mesa house until it sells."

"That will be more than a stretch," I say.

"It could be really difficult to sell."

"So, what do we need, my man?"

"We need a miracle."

"It's clear that God has been guiding our footsteps," I say.

"There's a scripture like that," he says. "It's Proverbs 3:6, 'In all your ways acknowledge him, and he shall direct your paths.' Remember when we prayed at the start of this project for him to open and close doors as he sees fit?"

"We'll have to listen carefully for his promptings."

He reaches across the table and squeezes my hand.

◆ ◆ ◆ ◆

Two weeks later, our La Mesa home is purchased "sight unseen" by an investor on the East Coast who wants to use it as a rental. For the very first time in our married life, we have a chunk of money in the bank.

"This is an answer to prayer, wouldn't you say?" Larry asks.

"'No good thing will he withhold from them that walk uprightly,' right? And it stands to reason that if the timing wasn't right, he would have put a kibosh on it. I kind of like how it turned out."

1989 SPRING BREAK

Feeling pretty flush, with some money in the bank, Larry decides to do the Wagner version of a *big splurge*. Honking a few times to get our attention, he turns into the driveway and waves wildly as he drives up in a brand-new station wagon, a woody.

Jumping up from the dining room table, where they are doing homework, the boys run to the sliding door and out onto the deck. "Oh, wow. Daddy, did you buy a new car?" Kyle asks.

"No, it's a rental, but I wanted to do something special to celebrate. Finish your homework and start packing, because as soon as you're done with your minimum day tomorrow, we are going on an adventure."

"Where, Daddy, where?" Kyle demands.

"Well, do you like baseball?"

"I love baseball," Brett says.

"OK, and do you like Tony Gwynn?"

"He's my favorite."

"Me too …"

"Me too …"

"Me too …"

"Would you like to see him in person?"

"Oh, yes, Daddy. Do we get to go to a game at the stadium?" Chad asks.

"I have something even better in mind for you. We are headed to the Yuma, Arizona, Padres spring training camp."

"Tony Gwynn will be there?" Chad wants to verify, just to be sure he's hearing what he thinks he is.

"Yep, and every other player on the Padres baseball team."

◆ ◆ ◆ ◆

It's a beautiful clear morning and we're all feeling pretty much like celebrities in this new station wagon.

"Do you want to stop somewhere really special on the way?"

"Where, Daddy, where?"

"On the way, there's a place called the Old Yuma territorial prison."

"Will there be prisoners there?" Ben wants to know.

"No, it's not in operation right now. It's more like an outside museum, and you can see what it's like to get right inside the cells. Should be fun for you guys, but you'd better behave because you sure don't want to end up in one of those prison cells."

"For real, Daddy?" Kyle asks, with a little hesitation in his voice.

"Don't worry, you guys," I say. "Would you believe me if I told you that I called ahead? Yeah, to tell them you'd be really well behaved. I'm sure we won't have any problems."

"Nuh-uh, Mommy," Brett insists.

Diverting them, I say, "You guys all got your swimsuits, right? Good, because we're staying at a place called the Days Inn and they have a swimming pool."

Finishing up the territorial prison visit, we decide to stop by the ball fields and check out the scene before checking into our room. It surprises us to see that we can sit in the boxes, only about an arm's length away from the players, just behind home plate.

As Dad is checking us in at the Days Inn, Kyle whispers to his brothers, "Hey, guys, isn't that Tony Gwynn?!"

And it is. Tony and all the members of our beloved Padres team were checking into the same motel we'd be staying in. I put a finger on each of my guys' shoulders as if to say, "Don't stare, give them their space."

Our room has two double beds for the six of us, a big step up from camping. After unpacking and negotiating the sleeping rotations for the next few days, we head to the popcorn and drinks happy hour as if we fit right in. After that, our guys jump in the pool right along with Tony Gwynn's kids. I am very proud of them for playing it down. But when Gwynn's kids keep looking back and forth at Chad and Ben, our identicals, then at Brett and Kyle, all of them towheads and about the same size, our family is the one getting the stares.

Chad is a consummate spokesperson and can't resist. He blurts out, "We are quadruplets. You know, the San Diego quadruplets—and that's why we look alike."

Everybody within earshot turns their head and stares. It seems we are immediately relegated to *star status*. And that's how the week starts. Tony's kids and ours think the other family is famous and worthy of awe, but they're all just kids, playing in the pool, watching the games, having a ball. My only regret is that being so busy with kids, I don't seem to be able to find time to connect with the adults. That's becoming a very common theme as time marches by.

The trip, every minute of it, has been a much-needed getaway. Baseball, autographs, restaurants, and pool time have been like water to a thirsty soul. However, all the loudness, commotion, and chaos is getting on my nerves. Some people seem to need solitude. I'm finding out I'm one of them.

◆　◆　◆　◆

Back home, the alarm rings at 5:30 a.m. I start the coffee, make sure everything necessary for the breakfast lineup is here, leave notes about what time everyone needs to be ready to go and what they need to take with them to school today—then

I head to my walk-in closet, my *prayer closet*, settle in with my coffee and prepare myself for the day at hand. The boys all know (and that includes Larry) that my time there is sacred, and that the day will go a lot more smoothly if that time is not interrupted. At first, it was awkward to be the unavailable mom and wife. But Larry is very supportive, and we have fallen into a positive routine that benefits us all.

My time spent with an ice turban wrapped around my head for the day is inversely proportional to the time spent in my prayer closet each morning before I take the kids to school.

LITTLE LEAGUE

If our guys weren't excited about Little League already, they certainly are now, after meeting Tony Gwynn and the whole Padres team in person a while back. Registering them for the season, I'm determined to have them all on the same team, just as they were with coach Malone in La Mesa T-Ball.

"We've never encountered a request like this before," the registrar says with some hesitation. "Four brothers on the same team … I don't think any of the coaches will agree to that."

"What will it take to make this work?" I ask.

"Well, maybe your husband would be willing to coach the team."

I know that can't happen, as he teaches at the music school every afternoon. Thinking for a moment, I quickly decide. I can do this. Without hesitation I blurt out, "I can do that!"

"What?"

"Well, my husband's not available, but I can do that. I can coach."

I notice that he and his cohort are hesitant. *They probably think I have no idea what I'm getting into, and I probably don't, but I'll learn. Maybe they'll figure this could end up being pretty entertaining for them. One way or another, I am not carting the boys around to four different practices every day.*

They agree to it, and I become the coach/manager of the team that has the four brothers and our neighbor Anthony. Later five others are added to the team, and off we go.

Baseball is something I've never played, but hey, I'd never put a house together before either, until I struck out and did it. I'll put a team together and they'll be tops when I'm finished.

Later, Anthony's dad Brian offers to be the manager and I pretend I know what he is talking about. *I know what it means to coach, but I don't know the concept of manager, yet.*

Our guys are sized for uniforms, a day is scheduled for the kids and their parents to meet their coach and manager, and we are off and running. After a quick study of baseball, I feel confident.

◆　◆　◆　◆

For the first practice, the dads come out to see what the *mother of the quads* is going to do. They shake their heads when they think I'm not looking, especially when I pull my full-length wardrobe mirror out of the box and lean it against the fence. With whiffle balls, they all practice tossing, catching, pitching, and playing the catcher position in front of the mirror. I believe all of the kids should learn to play each of the positions. That way they'll have a grasp of the big picture, and perhaps be less likely to complain if they don't get to play the position they'd hoped for.

It is clear to me that both Brett and Kyle are a bit more intense about baseball than either Ben or Chad. That's fine; they'll find their sport in due time. But I don't think I can put my own son, Kyle, at pitcher position, and his brother, Brett, at the catcher position, even though they are very strong there. That might look like I am playing favorites with my kids, another good reason to rotate the positions.

Our team is virtually injury-free until the day Brett begins to cautiously walk up for his turn to be on deck. His teammate, already on deck, suddenly takes a big step back and decides to swing a few more times. The worst happens. One of those practice swings catches Brett smack in the middle of his mouth, loosening his tooth and splitting his lip wide open, blood running down his chin.

Somebody takes over and we are off for the emergency room. Wow, cuts to the lip are very painful, but thankfully, heal quickly. With the help of a dentist and a plastic surgeon, Brett is told he'll be able to kiss just fine when he grows up. Within a couple of weeks, he is ready to play his position again.

Sometimes I wonder what's more important to the kids, the sport or the treats that follow the practices and the games. Our kids have grown accustomed to a judicious passing out of treats after the game. One day after a great win, Brett fills his catcher's helmet with candy and goodies. As he leaves the field, he encounters a chain hanging from pole to pole in the parking lot to keep cars off the field. Without a thought, he attempts to jump over the chain, but gives too much throttle to his jump and hits his lip with his knee, breaking it open in the very same spot the stitches had just been removed from.

Before we head off to the emergency room again, Brett points down at the treats that had fallen on the ground and insists that we gather them up for him before we leave.

25

THE BENCH

Larry's coming up the driveway. It's 7:15 p.m. When he walks in the door, I say, "Hey, babe, so glad you're home. Hungry?"

"Famished."

"How does Mexican yum yums sound?"

"Only like just about the best thing on the planet."

"I'll get the guys ready for *Little Visits with God* while you're chowing down, K?"

With the kids all hunkered down, we get in our jammies, grab a cup of ginger tea, and snuggle up on the sofa for our usual debriefing after a long day.

"I have something I'd like us to brainstorm on if you've got enough energy left. Is that OK?"

"Sure, lay it out there."

"I'm getting so tired of hearing the boys arguing and am trying to decide whether to intervene, referee, or just let it resolve itself. I mean, we have plenty of space now, but everyone seems to want to hang out in the family room. That's great, but when two of them *get into it* and the decibel level starts to shoot up through the ceiling, I feel like my head is going to explode. I'm tempted to send them into another room to have it out, but I'm also afraid of what the results might look like. How about if we have them go out of the family room and sit in the entry with their brother if they want to argue."

"That wouldn't help, would it, Janna? We'd still hear them, and that would be annoying."

"OK, hear me out. Let's take it up a notch."

"Go on."

"It's a little bizarre."

"Why am I not surprised," he says with a smirk.

"Picture it. They can argue, but they have to get up, walk out of the family room into the entry, sit on the bench side by side, with hands folded so they don't do bodily harm to each other."

"But their voices will still annoy us."

"Here's the ringer. They have to do their arguing in a *whisper*."

Larry gives a belly laugh, no doubt imagining how that will play out. "I'm willing to give it a try," he says, still laughing.

"OK then, let's let them know in the morning that we're going to have a family meeting when you come home from work tomorrow. Deal?"

"Deal. You know, I think this will be fun."

"Maybe they'll learn something about conflict resolution."

"Yeah, then maybe they can help you and me out with that one."

"Oh, very funny."

◆　◆　◆　◆

"OK, guys, we have a new plan to end the arguments—at least to make the arguments not drive us crazy. You are going to have to argue quietly," I say.

"How do you do that?" Ben asks.

"That's a great question, and we will tell you as soon as Mommy and Daddy act it out for you. Follow us into the entry so we can introduce you to the *arguing bench*."

"Isn't that the toy chest?" Chad asks.

"Well, yes, young man, it is indeed," Larry says. "But it is going to double as an arguing bench. Mom is going to tell you how it works."

"We all like to get the right answer, especially when it's a game, right? Sometimes we don't agree. So, what do we do when we don't agree?"

"We argue," Kyle says.

"Kyle and Brett argue a lot," Chad says.

"That's because Kyle argues at me," Brett says.

I look at Larry. "Looks like we have their interest, anyway." We both laugh.

"So back to the plan. Have you ever heard Mommy and Daddy argue?"

They all nod their heads. Their quick response saddens me. "Sometimes we disagree on something and we just talk about it. But sometimes we disagree about something and our voices start to get loud. When we disagree and talk really loud with each other, do you like it?"

"I don't like it when you yell," Ben says. "It makes me sad."

Boy, that really sends the message home to me.

"Can we agree that it would be better to disagree with each other without yelling?" I ask.

"Yes, Mommy, that would be much better," Chad says without looking directly at either of us.

"OK, here is how we're going to do this. Daddy and I have dubbed that bench the arguing bench. If two of you are going to argue, you need to go around the corner, sit on the bench side by side, and argue in a *whisper* until you resolve it."

Ben shoots up his hand. "What does 'resolve' mean?"

Larry puts his hand on my shoulder to let me know he will take this one. "It means to end the fighting with an answer you both agree on. Even if it means you agree to disagree. Both are winners, and we say it's a win-win. And so, it also means there is no loser. Sometimes you will agree, sometimes you won't. But once you resolve your argument, you're ready to do something that's more fun, like coming back into the family room to be with the gang, play the piano, run around outside—fun stuff like that. Sometimes it even means asking your brother to forgive you or saying that you're sorry for what you did or what you said."

Turning to me, he says, "Maybe we should act out an example for them, Jan. Let's disagree about something."

"Oh, doesn't that sound like fun?" I say sarcastically. "Let's do it."

"OK, guys," he says. "Sit down somewhere in the hallway and we'll show you what it looks like. The rules are that the two people have to sit right next to each other on the bench, with their hands folded in their lap. When we start talking, we must keep it at a whisper. If we raise our voices, we will have to get up, go in the other room for a five-minute time-out, and then start all over again. Does that make sense?"

They all nod.

"Here we go."

We ad-lib a little sketch of us arguing about getting the chores done, and about who is working the hardest, and what is fair. We keep it at a whisper, as they watch with rapt attention, finding it quite fascinating. *Now it's turning into a game that everyone wants to play.*

It works like a charm. And it is hilarious. Within two or three minutes, when a couple of them have been arguing in a whisper, at least one of them busts out laughing. The anger gets diffused and the conflict is either resolved or forgotten altogether.

◆　◆　◆　◆

This evening, after a week of using the arguing bench, Larry comes in late after the kids are already in bed. I never got a call from him to let me know he'd be late. I am miffed and I let him know it. He gets on the defensive and raises his voice. Pretty soon we're both going at it. We resolve it, but not without some seriously heated words toward each other.

In the morning, Ben is the first one to get to the kitchen for breakfast. He looks up at me and asks, "What do we do when you and Daddy are arguing and you get loud? It makes me feel scared and sad. Are you supposed to use the arguing bench too, or is it just us boys?"

I wrap my arms around him and ask him to forgive me for raising my voice. I tell him that Mommy and Daddy are no longer angry with each other, but that I'm glad he said something to me; we are working on it, but we need to try a little harder.

◆　◆　◆　◆

When the kids are off to school, I call our counselor Gordon Bear, now our friend. He leads marriage workshops with his wife, Bonnie.

"Hi, Gordon. Janna Wagner here. I've got something I'd like to run by you."

He starts by asking a few questions about Larry and me, to satisfy his concern that we were doing OK with each other. "What is on your mind, Janna?"

"I remember in that marriage workshop we did about a month ago, you gave us some how-to instructions to verify communication. Not sure I'm saying that right, but I bet you know what I mean."

"Yes, I know what you're referring to."

"I want to try some of those concepts on our kids to help them resolve conflicts. I came up with a mock conversation that I think might be helpful. Could I run it by you please?"

"Certainly."

"OK, here goes. The scenario is something like this: 'Ben, what do you hear your brother saying?' Ben responds. Then, turning to Chad, 'Chad, is that what you meant to say?' Am I on the right track?"

"We may have an opening for a counselor here," he says with a lilt in his voice. "So, yes. If they can gain that skill at this young age and keep using it, they will have the potential to be peacemakers. Most arguments that get out of hand have to do with both sides being understood. The critical components come down to listening, validation, and cooperation."

As time goes on, we teach them how to use some of the counseling skills we gain for resolving conflict. The added benefit is that we are improving our marriage communications as well. *God knows we need it.*

26

THE *DAILY CALIFORNIAN* NEWSPAPER

Lifestyles, January 22, 1992

Larry and I are sitting on the sofa, going over the article from the newspaper. I just read the intro and am continuing with the rest of the story …

As if the Wagner quadruplets' birth wasn't a big enough media event, now the family is filming an educational music series called The Quad Squad.

Chad, Ben, Kyle, and Brett are naturals in front of the camera. Newshounds don't faze the 10-year-old quadruplets, who are used to it by now. … The days and months following their birth were a media event. … The foursome's latest foray into the spotlight, however, is focused on their musicianship, not their rarity of siblings. The Wagner family has been busy filming a series of three educational videos called "Keep the Rhythm—with Professor Music and The Quad Squad." Filming was done in National City at Foursquare Productions on Friday.

As I read the article, I crack up at the disparity between the idyllic setup I'm reading about and the reality of how it really went down.

"It's true," I tell Larry. "All four are comfortable in front of the camera and not bugged by newshounds, but they sure were bugged by their brothers."

"What do you mean?" he asks.

"There was a moment during filming at 10 p.m. last week. Picture four ten-year-old brothers sitting shoulder to shoulder on wooden stools for more than four hours, with smiles pinned on their faces. They were all dressed up in their *Quad Squad* gear, sweat accumulating on their brow and rolling down their backs. The bright lights and cameras are pointed directly at them from about six feet away. They are being asked to smile 'a little bit more enthusiastically this time please.' But they clearly are no longer happy about this event. They begin poking at each other."

"I was spent too," Larry says. "That's when you asked the director for another break, right?"

"Yep. I said, 'Here you go, guys. Grab one of these damp washcloths and wipe yourself off again. I need to brainstorm on how to make this more fun for you.'"

"Jan, you always know how to make things work out. I have to hand it to you. You missed one thing, though. I was ready to throw in the towel at that point too, watching you pace back and forth for those three minutes. What was on that napkin you were showing the boys anyway?"

I reach into the table drawer and pull it out. "I'll read it to you because it's illegible. They're just bullet points, but I'll embellish it for your benefit."

Step one	Gather a whole bunch of one-dollar bills.
Step two	I put on a visor, the key tool I'll use to grab their attention.
Step three	I arrange the dollar bills to all stick out of the visor.
Step four	I wave my hand around wildly during filming while mouthing to the boys to smile at you, Professor Music.

"I told the boys, 'Here's how it works, guys. You get $1 for every five minutes that you stay enthusiastic and excited as we film. The one who is the most enthusiastic gets all the leftover treats when we're done!'"

Larry tilts his head and chuckles. "The line I remember you saying is *There's no such thing as overacting.*"

"Well, it was exactly the boost they needed right then. Don't you agree?"

"Maybe so, Jan, but watching you behind the cameras … I'd have to say you did sort of look like a circus clown. You kept holding up that sign that said, 'Smile' and 'Look Happy.' It must have made an impression on them, because they certainly didn't underact."

"Yeah, just wait till you see yourself on the screen. You weren't exactly an underactor yourself, dear."

We laugh.

WEEKS LATER—THE REVIEWS ARE IN

After dinner, we all gather in the living room with popcorn and the newspaper. Larry reads the highlighted sections about the project, now ready for distribution:

Accompanied by tapes and supplemental classroom materials like games and flash cards, the video-based curriculum is designed to help kindergarten through fourth-graders learn basic musicianship … The videos are expected to be available for nationwide release next month. … The State Department of Education has approved the materials, which cost $199.95 per classroom set.

The brothers all play music, and their father, Larry, is of course "Prof. Music." Janna and Larry Wagner operate Wagner's School of Music, a business that teaches comprehensive musicianship to 300 youngsters in four locations countywide.… The program, "Keep the Rhythm," contains materials and is intended for even the nonmusical teacher, who is often uncomfortable with teaching an unfamiliar subject.

"Here are the parts from the newspaper that I really want you guys to hear. Are you ready?"

Cheers of "Go, Quad Squad" fill the room.

Larry Wagner, 38, a music instructor for 15 years, said there is not much available right now in the way of quality, entertaining materials to teach music. … He figures there's good market potential for the video series. So far, he and his wife have invested $25,000 to produce them.

"Teachers know that music education is basic," he said. "A lot of elementary school teachers feel inadequate to present a program. But music education is mandated by the State. The justification for that is that study after study has shown music helps abstract thinking and coordination of right/left brain functions. It helps break up the intellectual activities (during the school day)."

He said the materials are not meant to replace the music specialist, rather they can lighten the specialist's workload or augment the curriculum when the school has no music specialist.

Teachers who piloted the curriculum liked it, calling it user-friendly and one that makes it easy and fun for children to take part in.

Professor Music's Quad Squad are fifth-graders and have been steeped in music from the age of four, starting with the piano.

Interest peaks when they hear the narrative shift to them personally.

At eight or nine, the boys could buy a second instrument with their own money. Chad and Ben also play electric guitar and the alto saxophone, respectively. Brett also plays the trumpet. Kyle chose to concentrate exclusively on the drums.

"These aren't like weirdo little musicians who live in a vacuum," said Janna Wagner. "These are like regular kids."

They make excellent grades, says their mother, and have been picked for the All-Star soccer team (American Youth Soccer Organization) two years in a row. … But it's not all smiles around the Wagner household, and the quads, predictably, aren't perfect angels.

"Sometimes it's rewarding and fun," Ben said about the mixed bag of being a quadruplet. "Everyone gets in fights. Some brothers say they are perfect; that's not true."

Children, as always, can be unkind—predictably targeting the unusual, or in this case, also the accomplished.

"Kids tease us to get a thrill out of it," said Chad. … Janna Wagner said jealousy may factor into both adult's and children's attitudes at times toward the family. After all, they may seem to have all the "right stuff." But a strong Christian faith is the family's anchor and guiding light, Janna Wagner said. Besides, she said, plenty of moms and dads struggle to raise their children, sometimes in difficult circumstances, and aren't showered with attention and praise for the job they do.

"The challenge of child-rearing increases exponentially," Janna Wagner said, admitting that she and her husband still date, their way of guarding against what she calls unhealthy parenting martyrdom.

"Sometimes I get kind of tired of it when I'm having a bad day," said Kyle of all the attention. "But I'm kind of used to it. It's kind of fun too."

The quadruplets began learning interpersonal communication skills at an early age—things their father said, jokingly, that he didn't learn until he was already married.

"Nobody's the boss, but everybody wants to be," Brett said.

As Larry puts the paper down and smiles, Chad stretches his arms while trying to minimize a yawn.

"Wow, Dad," says Chad. "That was good. Can we watch the Science Channel now?"

"Wait," says Dad. "Don't you guys want to talk a little about the article?"

"Not that much," Kyle says.

Selling the Idea —Circulation of the Videos

It's one thing to do video production and quite another thing to actually make some sales of the product. That's when I kick it into gear, calling nearly all of the school districts in a fifty-mile radius of our music school. Getting my foot in the door starts with "Hi, I wonder if you saw any of the news pieces regarding that family that had quadruplets?" That generally opens the door. Then after a pause, I say, "I'm the momma in that scenario." I go from there and the sales are fair, especially in the Camp Pendleton school district area.

Sales continue to rise until I visit a district where the superintendent tells me, "These days, you're expected to have a multicultural cross-section of actors in the scenes."

My brow wrinkles. "I'm confused. This is a family endeavor with the hook being the Quad Squad, who are all brothers … from the same family."

"Most every school in California will require that."

Clearly, that can't be our children, as they are all from one family.

We decide to do what any good entrepreneur would do when faced with this situation. We adapt. Larry comes up with *Professor Music and His Multicultural Band.* Musicians from a variety of cultures and countries come to the music school and record with Larry and the kids—teachers and musicians with roots in the Philippines, Mexico, Africa, and even Europe. We meet wonderful people in the making of it.

Larry has developed a fascination for dialects, accents, and traditional folk songs. When we are out and about, if we hear somebody speaking what seems to be Tagalog (a Filipino dialect), we softly begin to sing, *Magtanim ay di biro, Maghapong nakayuko.* They invariably look at us and laugh, saying, "How did you know that song?"

It's a simple song, sung by many Filipino children. Kind of like how many American kids learn "Mary Had a Little Lamb." It creates an immediate connection that he would know such a basic but popular song. The same goes for the Nigerian song, "Funga Alafia," or songs from Mexico, and on occasion, a Native American song, "Ya Ho Ya Hey."

Is our family enriched by the development of Professor Music and His Multicultural Band? Most certainly. Is there a profit in keeping with the effort and finances necessary to develop it? Depends on how you define profit. *Maybe our job is to just plant some seeds.*

27

11-YEAR-OLD'S ROLE REVERSAL

April 1993

We are on the road to visit Tahquitz Canyon in Palm Springs—the same testing place Larry expected me to climb in 1976, a sort of *qualification audition* for a potential lifetime mate. Now it's time to share it with our sons.

When we arrive, Larry gathers all of us around him to review the safety rules before we get started.

"OK, guys, this is going to be quite a stretch for you, but I know you're up to it. After the first waterfall, it gets steep. There are very few handhold grips on the canyon walls and boulders. Let's check to be sure we're ready and understand the climbing norms. Who can tell me what scrambling is?"

Kyle chimes in. "It means you're just using your body to climb—you're not using ropes and harnesses. You just have to rely on your own hands, legs, eyes, and all the rest of you to be safe."

"That's pretty good, Kyle. And what have I told you we need to watch for as we're going up a rock face?"

"Rattlesnakes," Brett says.

"That's right. Rattlesnakes. We also need to be careful of loose rocks and wet, slippery moss. Lastly, watch out for the crazy people who will practically run around you, wanting to go fast. Don't feel rushed, just take your time. It's not a race to see who gets there first. Are we clear on that one?"

They nod.

Larry and I check that all shoes are well tied, water bottles are in place, and that there is a good dose of climbing powder on everyone's hands—which they think is pretty cool.

Seeing some uneasiness in my guys' eyes, I remind them that "If you make plenty of scuffling noise, the critters will get out of your way before you get to them and you'll be safe. Remember, they are afraid of you. You are the big guys."

"Oh, and one more thing, guys," Larry chimes in. "If you accidentally drop something, just let it fall. Don't try to grab it—unless, of course, it's Mom."

"Oh, ha ha, aren't you funny?" I say. "I will be just fine. You just wait and see."

We climb up the outer face near the first falls easily. There's a narrow mountain goat path from there along a break of the mountain. The pools above the first falls look inviting, so Larry suggests we hike down and check them out. Larry is out front and informs us to be extra careful as the way down is rather steep. After we start our descent, I feel more and more uneasy. I brush the feeling aside, wanting very much to stay in the game, but Larry can sense my fear. "Wait there, guys. I'm gonna spot Mom, then we'll have you guys come down one at a time to join us. Just be patient."

He slips down onto a ledge with a good foothold and directs me to get on my belly and do the same.

"I have a spot all ready for you. Don't worry, I'll be right here."

As I begin to lower my body, I'm reassured by his hands on my hips guiding me. When I reach the landing, he reevaluates the area. Even though it's not a sheer wall, he decides it's not safe to continue going down.

Shouting up to the guys, he says, "Hold on, guys. This isn't going to work. I need to find a way to go out and around this spot before we go further."

As I wait, I lean into the face of this slanted wall. I close my eyes and grasp the moss and roots as fear continues to rise.

Shortly, Larry reappears and says, "Sorry, babe. It's a dead end. We'll just have to go back up the slope." There is a pause. "Jan, did you hear me? We're going to have to retrace our steps and go back up."

He is behind me, but when he gives me the go-ahead to start climbing, it hits me. My heartbeat quickens, my eyes tear up, and I feel panic overtake me.

"I can't move. I just can't do it," I confess through a tear. "I've lost my confidence to reach out to the sparse grips." Moving back upward looks impossible, and I feel stuck.

Larry comforts me, promising it will work out, as he puts his mind to work figuring out a way to get us all out of there safely. He instructs our boys to come down closer to where we are, spread out in a vertical row above me, and lay on their bellies, one above the other. Each is to grasp a handhold and foothold on the rock while using their free hand to hold onto the pant leg of the boy above them. Then he instructs me to just close my eyes and start climbing up over our sons. One, then another, then another, and then another.

They become a human ladder for me, and it gets me back to the goat path. Next, the boys just climb up, one over the other until they get to my location. Finally, Larry joins all of us. It's then that I open up the floodgates and weep as they rub my back and comfort me, reassuring me that everything is going to be OK.

When I can finally speak coherently, I turn my head toward Larry, "I wasn't ready for that."

"It was my fault putting you in that precarious situation," he says. "Please forgive me. I'm just glad you're OK."

"I forgive you."

As we make our way back, an onlooker pats my shoulder as I brush by, on our way to the van.

"You are an incredibly lucky lady," she says. "There was a helicopter rescue here yesterday." As she shuffles along quickly, catching up with the other younger people in her group, I ask in a raised voice, "Wait, what's this about a helicopter rescue yesterday? Man or woman?"

"A man," she says over her shoulder.

"And where?"

"Right where you and your family were climbing up over each other. Gotta go, bye." Her voice trails off as I stop in my tracks, stunned. "Wait, you guys. Did you hear that?"

"Yes," Larry says. "Like I told the kids, you've got to be very careful and take your time, which is exactly what we did. When I was in Palm Springs High School, helicopters were up here nearly every weekend."

"And *now* you're telling me this?"

"Well, I always thought it was because the pot smokers and partiers did stupid stuff, which a lot of them did, and ended up falling and needing rescue. But today we managed to get into a bind even with all our wits about us."

"Wow … and as the girl said, it was at the very same spot where I had struggled today! Thank you, sons, for watching out for my well-being. You may just have saved my life today. I'll never forget it!"

PART FOUR

28

UH-OH

Full-on adolescence is staking its claim. *Hardy Boys* books and *choose-your-own-ending* books are now considered passé, and fake *making out* with stuffed animal Puffalumps (kissing practice) is a thing of the past. They are getting dangerously close to wanting that first real kiss. Yikes!

It's a school night, and the kids are all hunkered down for a decent night's sleep before the testing they'll all be doing tomorrow.

Larry and I snuggle for a few minutes on the sofa, then he reaches for the channel changer.

"Hold on a minute," I say. "I want to ask you something."

"OK, shoot."

"What do you think about this whole adolescence thing?"

"What do you mean?"

"I'm thinking it seems like sheer torture for kids. I mean, I'm a girl, so I'm well aware of the feelings girls have, but I had no idea that boys could get so testy, confused, frustrated, irritable, disrespectful, sad, defiant, and just plain hard to live with. Were you like that at this age?"

He shrugs his shoulders.

"I mean, it seems like they're all going through it in one way or another," I persist.

"Think of it this way," he says. "They have each other and they have their faith. Imagine how difficult it might be if they were all alone in their misery."

"You make a good point. Anyway, I'm thinking about going back to school so I can be a middle school teacher."

"What, are you insane?"

Now I have his full attention. "No, not completely. But I know what it is to feel sad, and I know what depression feels like, and rage as well. Think how irrational you and I get when we're duking it out verbally. Sometimes we don't even know what we're arguing about. For sure we each want very much to be understood. Imagine how hard it is for these kids who might not even have learned how to rein in their emotions."

"Let's be honest, Janna. Do you and I know how to rein in our emotions?"

"Guilty as charged. But I'd like to learn."

"Don't you think you'd be overcommitting by becoming a teacher? The years of schooling, then student teaching, and then subbing—all before you get hired in a permanent position."

"I thought about that, and it is a concern. But here's the thing. This might sound arrogant, but I feel like I'm getting a calling from God to do this thing."

"I won't argue against you on that point," he says. "Perhaps we should pray about it as a couple, then if it seems right, you can step forward and make a move in that direction, and evaluate it along the way—see how it sits with us."

"You'd be agreeable? Just like that?"

"I remember what we said in our marriage vows, 'that we may with one mind and one mouth glorify God our Father.'"

"Oh, Larry, you are a rare man indeed."

"We'd have to get a loan for your classes along with whatever we can kick in. Let's keep it in prayer, and if all the doors open, we'll take it as a sign."

"I do feel really concerned about adolescent kids. I mean, I just want to be a part of helping them survive this time of borderline insanity until they get on the other side of it. Sometimes people just want to root for the underdog, and that's me."

1994—National University and Mom's Saga

"So, you're going to be a student too?" asks Brett.

"Yep, and a middle school teacher. We'll all be going through the student thing together."

I jump on the fast track at National University in San Diego, to finish my courses and secure my teaching credential. Thus begins the era of the mom who shows up at every one of my sons' events with a clipboard and a pile of my own assignments to complete. In time, it's with papers to grade, or lesson plans to make whenever and wherever we go, including their music rehearsals, soccer games, tennis matches, diving matches, cross-country races, football games, and against my better judgment, even driving my boys around town to find the best aggressive skating spots. My head isn't always up, but at least I am close by, which gives me great peace, though it may bug them to have Mom around so much.

They'll have to wait until they're old enough to drive to have more independence. Oh, God, the thought of them driving terrifies me.

◆　◆　◆　◆

I secure enough credits to get a multi-subject credential and begin my hunt for employment.

Within a few weeks of subbing, I get a request to interview for a position at an elementary school. The interview panel likes me and I like them. I think the part about the *mother of quadruplets* kind of gets their attention.

How hard can this be? After all, I'll only have fifteen students in my classroom.

I kind of gloss over the part in my mind where they say that it is a class for severely emotionally disturbed children. I seem to have a habit of underrating the challenge of certain situations.

On my first day, a chair is thrown across the room at me by one of my students. *Is this a wake-up call? I've been granted an emergency credential for teaching special education based on my agreeing to enroll in a master's degree program while teaching this particular class. I'd better figure out how to make it a success.*

I focus on making my boundaries clear, consistent, and reasonable. The kids begin to respond well to me. When the San Diego Chargers football team gets a chance to go to the Super Bowl, my students think it will be fun to make their logo (a lightning bolt) into snap-on pins that they can sell to their parents. Word gets out on campus, and they can hardly keep up with the demand for the 25-cent yellow bolts. The Chargers don't win, but the students get a taste of success and a little lesson in entrepreneurialism. It boosts their morale and makes it a lot easier for me to teach math concepts, using that experience as a reference point.

◆　◆　◆　◆

As the 1995 school year begins, I transfer to a school closer to our kids' high school. It's easy for them to walk the one mile from their high school to my new classroom after they've completed their sports and music activities. I teach a middle school special day class for students with mild learning disabilities.

It troubles me that some of these 11- to 13-year-olds cannot yet read. I find a great reading program and determine that no child will leave my classroom without having learned to read. That works out very well. One grandmother, charged with raising her grandson, is so grateful that when she decides to get rid of her motorhome, she gives it to our family in gratitude. Our sons are going to have many outings in that motorhome in the years ahead!

Behavior Modification, Tried and True

"How did you sleep last night, honey?" Larry asks.

"Not well. I'm so nervous. It's just so completely foreign to me. And some of what she says so far is hard for me to grasp."

"Well, Jan, she's meant to be your coach, right?"

I nod.

"So she's on your side. Ann wants the best for you. I'm sure you'll do just fine."

"I wish you could be invisibly present so that I didn't have to face it alone. It would be pretty weird for you to go to the meeting with me, right?"

He nods in agreement. "Break a leg."

"How about you pray for me?"

"You got it, babe. God, please give Jan the confidence of knowing you are right there with her, and that she is your child, following your direction. Allow her to reflect you and your spirit as she meets with Dr. Solomon. Amen."

◆　◆　◆　◆

"Hi, Mrs. Wagner," Dr. Solomon says with a smile. "Come on in. I'm excited to see what you settled on for your thesis topic." She points to the chair I'm to sit in. We are in the professor's second-story office at National University, Mission Valley, San Diego.

"We are on track, so your master's thesis is the final requirement for getting your master's degree. First of all, do you have any questions?"

"Yes, Dr. Solomon, I have several. I've never written a master's thesis before."

"That's usually the case," she says with a gentle smile.

"You said that we should construct our thesis around a specific subject that we have a personal passion for, if at all possible."

She nods.

"You recall that I have quadruplet sons. The thing is, there's pretty much nothing I'm as passionate about as those four kids of mine."

"Well then, you are extremely fortunate. A great many students walk in this door for this meeting with absolutely no idea what they want to research for their thesis. I'd say you have a real edge there."

"Oh, that is very encouraging. So, here I go. In following the directives you gave me at our last meeting, if I heard correctly, the title should be very specific, clear, and precise, leaving the reader with no question at all about the goal I have for my project."

"Yes, that's right."

"I believe you also said that it's not necessary to have a catchy title, as long as you are clear about what your subject matter is. So here I go …"

"I can hardly wait. Please, go ahead."

"The title is 'Chore Completion by 13-year-olds: A Behavior Modification System to Increase Frequency of Chores Without Verbal Reminders.'"

Dr. Solomon closes her eyes for a few moments, deep in contemplation.

"That's a wonderful title. Have you started your research perchance?"

"Yes. I was so excited about it that I went ahead and researched the literature."

"Do you have that piece with you today?"

"Yes, and I've given some serious consideration about how to quickly implement it, for the benefit of our children, and frankly, for my sanity. I hope that's OK that I jumped ahead."

◆　　◆　　◆　　◆

In four weeks, after implementing my idea and submitting my thesis to Dr. Solomon, she calls me to come back into her office before graduation, saying that I should see about getting my work published.

Alas, somehow I don't think I'll find the time or energy to follow through on the publishing. *I'm just thrilled that all four of our sons now complete their chores without verbal reminders.*

◆　◆　◆　◆

The strategies I used for my thesis have been put to good use in our own home. There is a chore chart on the refrigerator that each son tracks daily to check off chores completed. I began by reminding them of their chores and rewarding them with a dime for each chore completed. After the first week, I left the remembering to them, rewarding them with the dime only if the chore was completed on time, without verbal reminders. If they forget to do their chore, they must pick up one of their brothers' chores the next day along with their own chore. All that without the joy of receiving a dime.

Today, Kyle is telling me that the only thing he doesn't like about the chore chart is what happens when he forgets to do his chore. "Like last week when you turned to Chad and said, 'Hey, Chad, which of your chores would you like Kyle to do for you tomorrow?'"

"That probably makes you mad and frustrated, right? But I notice you did all of your chores on time the next day, didn't you?"

"Of course! I'm not about to let him have that satisfaction a second time."

"Exactly," I say, as I give him a big hug.

29

BOYS AT 14 YEARS: SUMMER BEFORE FRESHMAN YEAR OF HIGH SCHOOL

"OK, son. Tell me about this master plan you and Kyle came up with for the basement, and how you guys implemented it. I seem to have been working diligently for so long now that I've missed a lot."

"It's all right, Mom," Chad begins.

"You know, son," I say, "I'm not sure it's ever worth missing some of your own son's childhood like I have this year."

"Mom, I'm not really a child anymore. We're in high school now. And it's almost summer."

Bam! How'd that happen? I kind of wish time would slow down a minute here. "Good point, so tell me about it."

"I really got into guitar this summer, when I started learning Jimi Hendrix and fell in love with his music, playing for like eight hours a day in the all-dirt basement."

I scrunch up my face and say, "Are you going to say it's creepy down there? And there are spiders?"

"Guys don't care about that stuff," he reminds me. "Sometimes we just want to be alone and make as much noise as we want to, doing what we love. Who cares if the floor is dirt? Not me, that's for sure. I mean, I know someday you and Dad will get the downstairs finished, but I want a place to do music right now, so I think I've got a great setup."

Larry and I have plans to make space for a stairwell and fulfill our dream of doubling the square footage of our home, with the downstairs having two bathrooms and four bedrooms. But the money isn't here yet and Chad isn't about to let that stop him from having a practice room.

Chad continues. "Jimi Hendrix is so good, but his riffs are really hard to play and it takes lots of practice. It would drive you nuts if I play the guitar that much upstairs. I get to play 'The Star-Spangled Banner' at the opening of a basketball game in a few weeks, and I'm going to play it Jimi Hendrix style. I'll have to really have it nailed."

"You know, you might blow some minds with that version," I warn.

"If I do it right, and clean, they'll like it."

Some things he's hesitant about. But, when it comes to his music, he's all-in, and right now, he's passionate about it.

"See that pile of stuff down there, Mom?" he continues as he points to a corner in the basement.

I nod.

"Underneath that pile of blankets is an amp."

"You don't say."

"Yeah, Dad let me set up down here so I can practice. It's true, I've been doing that like six to eight hours a day while you're out. Remember I told you I wanted to form a pep band?"

"Huh? Vaguely," I say.

"For pep band, Ryan, Brett, and some other guys come over. It's fun. We just pretty much play whatever we want to play—rock 'n' roll, baby."

"I don't remember hearing a whole bunch of guys playing down there in the basement."

"Yeah, Dad said it would be better if we had those guys over when you weren't home. He jumps in and joins us sometimes. Dad's a pretty good musician."

"You don't say."

"Kyle gets into it too. Once, Dad even hauled down his Fender Rhodes piano for us. Kyle puts a lot of his incredible energy into coming up with drum riffs for the band he hopes to form one day. You know he loves to accompany himself on piano too, as he sings his original songs at the top of his lungs, right? (I nod.) Vince, on the music crew at church, said that Kyle could never walk past a piano anywhere without sitting down and playing it, kind of like Dad."

"Gee, I appreciate you explaining to me how this whole thing in the basement evolved. I agree that you have a really good setup. And now, I'm feeling just a tiny bit concerned about the neighbors."

TWEENERS

Early on a Saturday afternoon, alone on the living-room sofa, Ben surfs the channels in one of those rare moments when there is nobody to argue with him about what show will go on the screen. On weekday afternoons he and his brothers are limited to watching the Science, Discovery, and National Geographic channels, per the Wagner household boundaries. But today is Saturday, so with his soccer match finished, homework complete, and his brothers scurrying to get their chores and homework done, he's the king of the remote. He settles into an episode of *Saved by the Bell* as I gather up the remainder of the laundry that didn't quite make the target as it was tossed into the laundry baskets.

Pushing my stacked laundry baskets across the tile floor toward the family room, I call out, "Ben, any more laundry you need to add?"

Silence. *Maybe he didn't hear me. I call out again. Still no response. Is he ignoring me?*

"Ben, do you hear me?"

"What?" he responds with an edge, as he turns his head to finally acknowledge me.

It feels like I'm interrupting a lion at mealtime.

He gets up and passes by me without a word or eye contact. As he quickly heads back to his room to gather up his dirty clothes, I realize that this attitude of defiance from the boys is raising its ugly head more and more frequently. Chad and Brett are often dismissive, sometimes complying, but often only with a reminder, and then without eye contact, with an air of dismissal. I don't see them responding that way to their dad, but for sure, I am no longer held in the high regard or respect of *Sergeant Mommy*, who was always greeted with a smile and a measure of enthusiasm about being cooperative. Those days are gone. I'm sad but think better of making a thing of it just yet. After all, I do live in a home with five boys, four of whom are teenagers. *Maybe there is some commonality about this scenario that I can learn something about before confronting the tribe.* Just as I'm swallowing that lump in my throat, Kyle comes into the room and gives me the hug I need.

When Kyle sits on the sofa with Ben, the conflicts begin. "I want to watch tennis now, Ben."

"Too bad, I was here first."

"But that's not fair. You've had all this time to watch whatever you want to. It's my turn now."

He turns to me. "Mom, Ben's being arrogant."

Larry walks into the room, saving the day as he begins to roughhouse with the both of them. The screams of excitement and joy are more than Brett and Chad can resist. They both open their doors and run out. Now four teenagers are wrestling together with Dad. That's about 700 pounds of testosterone. Trying to adhere to my self-imposed standard of not correcting my husband in front of my children, I decide it's best to leave the room and find another place to hang out.

When I return from a run around the property with Dusty, our dog, their male bonding is complete, at least for the moment. *Do I have to join in the wrestling to maintain my position in the tribe? Or would that even make a difference?* After a dinner of Mexican yum yums, we wrap it up with Mom's oat bars covered with plenty of ice cream, whipped cream, and a cherry on top.

◆　◆　◆　◆

It's movie night. Last week the gang appeased me by queuing up my all-time favorite, *Princess Bride.* There were lots of belly laughs and reciting of longtime memorized lines by all as we watched, often putting the screen on pause as every person did their rendition of some such line as "Have fun storming the castle" or, "As you wish."

Tonight, we're back to the usual—some sort of boy movie, the likes of which I often refer to as a *Ridiculous, Reptilian-Minded Sci-Fi* (usually not uttered out loud). Tonight, it's *Terminator II*, for the ninth time.

I open the folding door of my 5 × 7-foot quilting closet, conveniently located adjacent to the family room. I can feign interest and be in the proximity of my guys as I use my drafting board, turned sewing table, to quilt away to my heart's delight. I've lovingly named my hobby quilt therapy. Everyone's happy and no one is left out. Now and then I make a real effort to get into the plot of their sci-fi show, but it just doesn't work for me, no more than the effort of buying fabric, cutting it into little squares, and then sewing it back together again would make sense to any one of my guys.

Partway through *Terminator II*, I raise my head and laugh as I hear, right on cue, "I'll be back," followed by Larry's rendition, "You be Bach, I'll be Beethoven." My eyes involuntarily roll, as I have no control over this reaction when it comes to lines and jokes during any sci-fi.

◆　◆　◆　◆

We get to church early Sunday morning so the guys can get set up with the high school worship band. Larry and I make our way up two flights of stairs to the Young Families class, scheduled to have a well-known guest and an open forum for questions and answers. "I am so ready for this, honey," I say. "I have so many questions about this transition time our kids are living through, especially about the attitudes teenage boys have with their moms as they awkwardly find their way into manhood."

"Awkward? I hadn't noticed that."

"Well, that's the thing. You're one of the guys, so maybe you don't notice it. But I'd wager that most of the moms might be going through the same stuff as I am, with the lack of respect and loss of the warmth and kudos our sons used to give. I feel that they all have an underlying conflict going on that I can't put my finger on."

◆　◆　◆　◆

By the end of the hour, I have a lot better understanding of how difficult it is for many sons to break loose of their ties to Mom as they connect more and more with Dad in their efforts to grow into men. The speaker suggests that it can take a chunk of time for some boys to get comfortable enough at being a young man, while still having room in their circle for Mom. They seem to be more comfortable with Dad during adolescence. He stressed and acknowledged that it can be very painful for some moms and that they need a lot of support and outright affirmations from their husbands to get through this season.

Apparently, I'm not the only mom in our group to put her head into her pillow most nights and shed a few tears.

"Come here, honey. Let me hold you," Larry says when we get to the bottom of the stairs on our way out.

I have so much bottled up inside me for so long that all I can do is sniffle away as he caresses and reassures me.

Lord, help me to trust you as I walk through this season of my life. I know that the path that lies ahead of me is something you already know. And in my best moments, I abandon my worry and feelings of rejection to you and your care. Help me to trust you more.

◆　◆　◆　◆

As on most mornings, I find myself in my prayer closet. The boys are going through their usual routine of getting ready for school. There are plenty of clunking sounds coming from the bedrooms and an atmosphere of general commotion. Four showers, four breakfasts, four dishwasher openings, a few light arguments as well as the usual bantering. I wrap it up and come out so that we can all say our "I love yous," then it's blowing kisses as they open the family room door and start their run down the canyon toward the bus stop. Larry sits down at the piano in the dining room to play as I watch their images grow smaller and smaller until they make that turn to join our neighbor's kids at the bus stop.

I walk to the living-room sofa and curl up to listen to him for a while. As he gets more and more into his music, I get more and more into wondering *What might help our family to bond at this critical adolescent season?*

It occurs to me that we might benefit by doing something fun together that puts us all on a level playing field. Rock climbing comes to mind. I love heights, and I do get an adrenaline rush when I'm climbing. That one little scare with the human ladder was an exception, and I'm past it, now that I've felt the grip of climbing shoes and have a good sense of what my limits are. With spring break right around the corner and no plan in sight, it's a perfect opportunity for me to shine and be like one of the guys as things used to be.

As Larry wraps up his first original song, he turns and looks at me before segueing into his next creation. *He is a performer, for sure, and loves an audience, even if it's just his adoring wife.*

He turns to glance at me, checking out my response. I smile, and I'm sure my eyes are twinkling.

"What?" he asks.

"What do you mean?" I respond.

"I mean, why are you looking at me like that?"

"Because I love you, of course."

"But what else? You have that look on your face, and we had that big fight last night."

"OK, you read me too well. I'm over that fight, and we both apologized and forgave each other, but it seems like we might need a little bit of mending from the words we shouted. I have an idea brewing. I think it's time for us to go camping."

"Where do you have in mind?"

"I'll get back to you later on that."

We both smile and say, "I love you."

30

SPRING BREAK
—SERENDIPITY

1996

Two weeks later, riding along in the van, Chad and Brett are heavily into *The Daily Bread* magazine, admiring the extreme skaters' tricks as they thumb through it. Kyle is fully steeped in his book, *The Inner Game of Tennis.*

Ben looks up from his most recent sci-fi book in the Foundation series. He points out the window and says, "Look at this place, guys. It looks like something from a sci-fi movie."

"Or maybe even Mars," Kyle chimes in.

"OK then, sons. Get your noses out of your reading and let's have a look at our campsite," Larry says. "It's Jumbo Rocks Campground, number 115—should be right up here around the corner."

Brett is the first one out of the van, leaving his gear to pick up later. "Oh my gosh, it feels like an oven. It must be like 100 degrees or something."

"Trust me," says Dad. "The afternoon is the worst part, but it will cool off a bit later, and will stay light until about 8:00 p.m. We'll have time to set up camp and do a little hiking, maybe even some climbing when it cools off a bit."

Chad and Ben start making plans while setting up camp, and I start dinner on our Coleman stove. "Hey, Dad," Chad calls out. "Can we take a ride on the mountain bikes after dinner and get an idea of the lay of the land?"

Brett grabs Chad's elbow and looks at him, then at Dad. "Better yet, can we ride our skates?"

"Sure," says Dad. "Sounds like a plan: two on blades, two on bikes. You good with that, Janna?"

"Definitely. You guys are going to see some cool things, like tarantulas even."

"Like the ones we have in Jamul sometimes?" Brett asks.

"Yes, but a lot bigger and a lot more of them than you're used to. Just don't freak out if you startle one of them and it starts hopping all over the place. That's what they do when they think they're in danger. It can freak you out if you don't know it's coming—but they rarely bite."

"And what about those Joshua trees?" Brett chimes in. "It looks like if you fell into one of 'em, it would cut you all up."

"So it would, son. Look at all those rock formations. They're all over the place, and it looks like they'll make for a great bouldering time."

◆　◆　◆　◆

After skating, biking, and climbing, it's close to dinnertime. Kyle walks back into the campground after visiting the primitive toilet down the way. "Hey, guys, I talked to this guy down the road and he told me that Joshua Tree National Park is like the climber's nirvana."

"Well, let's just see about that," Larry says. "How's that dinner going, honey?"

I turn and smile. "Let's eat!"

Four days later

Tired, hungry, with injuries limited to scratches and bug bites, the six of us are all ready for a hot shower and a soft bed. As we finish breaking camp, the boys begin to haggle about who gets what seat on the way home.

"Take a walk and figure it out, guys," Larry says.

As I'm shoving the loose gear into the van, Larry begins to load the bikes. Just as he's securing the last one, two men in a small black compact pull up to our spot and open the window.

"Are you guys leaving?"

"Yeah, do you need our spot?" Larry asks.

"Yeah, but take your time."

"Feel free to start unloading your stuff if you want."

"Thanks, man. Actually, we don't have much gear, as you can see. But we'll go ahead and set our chairs down."

Larry does a double take.

The man continues. "I guess you notice my face is pretty well messed up," he says, as he starts climbing out of the car. "I got pretty beaten up by a guy who pulled me out of my car, then carjacked me."

"What a drag! Did you get your car back?"

"No, it's a goner. I just needed to get away for a while. My friend David here drove me up from LA. I'm Rob."

"I'm Larry, and this is my wife Janna." We all shake hands. "Our kids are out running off some steam."

In the distance, our guys advertise their imminent return, kicking up rocks and stirring up the dust, singing the lyrics of a heavy metal song, playing their invisible instruments. *I know they are imagining that they have a huge crowd of fans watching them.*

"Here they come," Larry says.

"Man, how many kids do you have anyway?!"

"There are four boys. I'll introduce you to them in just a second."

I give them the cue to settle down, as Larry moseys over to join Rob and David, signaling that it is time for guy talk.

When I walk over to give these two guys a soda, I hear Rob talking about being a music producer/agent, and that he'd written some songs of his own. It was torture to walk away from the conversation, but I know Larry will fill me in later. As I pull myself away, I hear Rob refer to also being something like a recording and a talent artist/manager.

They wrap it up, exchange names and contacts, and Larry buttons up the van and climbs in. With the kids all settled for the trip home, I finally get to hear the story. We speak in muted voices, not wanting to get the boys keyed up about some crazy dreams they might have about being performers.

"You know how it is," Larry starts. "I tried to be friendly. I told them our guys are quadruplets, and they found that interesting."

"You guys were talking for a long time. Humor me, and lay it all out."

"Yeah, well … I told him what we do for a living, that we have a music school for kids, that our kids have played piano since they were five years old, and that they sing."

"And?"

"He seemed interested, so I shared that they each play a couple of instruments. He didn't share much about himself; he just seemed interested in hearing our story, so that's it. And now we're headed home to jump back on the fast track. Let's keep this to ourselves, OK?"

Two weeks later, Larry calls a family meeting.

"Mom shared with me about how high school can be tough sometimes. Would you guys feel better about things in high school if you were sharing your music in the limelight, on the big stage?"

"What do you mean, Dad?" Kyle asks incredulously.

"I got a call from the music agent we met at Joshua Tree, Rob." He waits in silence to gauge their interest level, which became very clear, very quickly.

"What?"

"Wait?"

"Are you telling me …?"

"Tell us."

"Rob said he was sitting at home and it dawned on him that I had said you boys could sing. He thought that maybe he should follow up on that. Would it lift your mood to know that he might consider signing you if you can sing on pitch, sing harmonies, and show energy on the stage?"

Eyes are popping out of their sockets now as Larry describes the conversation he's just had.

"Rob says that the world needs a new boy band and that a band of four brothers, quadruplets even, would be an ideal and total hook. You just need to show him that you can sing and stay on pitch. He wants a cassette tape with you guys doing a song in four-part harmony. If you can do it, he thinks we just might have a deal. Should I start looking for a song for you guys?"

They all nod.

"We won't let this interfere with your education, so get to your homework while I try and figure out a good song for you. Chop-chop."

All six of us smash into a group hug, jumping up and down, excited about the possibility.

"Enjoy the moment, but show us that you can keep your head on in the midst of it."

◆　◆　◆　◆

Larry decides on the song "In the Still of the Night." After giving the boys their individual parts on cassette, it's time to put it together. They gather around the piano and he plunks out each of their parts ad infinitum, first individually, then as an ensemble. Four boys, four-part harmony, and all a cappella (no accompaniment). He figures that way Rob can hear the quality of their voices and the pitch without distraction. He sends the cassette off to Rob in Hollywood and we hold our breath, praying.

We get a call back after a few days.

"Oh my gosh," Rob tells Larry, "the boys can sing! They're rough and will need some grooming. But if you're interested in signing them, I'm interested in drawing up the papers. Let me send you a cassette for a cover song that might show off their talents a bit more than the one you had them sing. It's a Jackson 5 song. They got a lot of playtime with it. It's called 'Stop the Love.'"

"OK, Rob, that's great. They will be so excited, and we'll get the song down within a few days," Larry says.

"So, Larry, we'll have the boys come up here to Hollywood at some point and we'll sign some papers. I only take 15% of what the boys make, and I don't ask for any money from you up front. I'll be straightforward with you. If all goes well, I think this could be big. Four brothers all the same age and good-looking too. To be honest, even if the boys could barely sing, it wouldn't matter since we can fix that in the studio, but the fact they can sing, keep a beat, and sing on pitch, well, they have real talent. So all in all, I believe they have a winning combination going for them."

"Sounds good. I'll be looking for that tape and we'll work on it."

"All right, brother. Talk to you soon."

◆　◆　◆　◆

Larry gets the tape of "Stop the Love" from Rob and works with the boys on the parts. He mixes in their voices on an overdub and sends it back to Rob. Some time passes. Just as the boys get their focus back on high school sports and academics, Rob calls back.

"It sounds great," he says. "I want you to bring the family up to LA so we can sign the contract. At the same time we'll meet up to do a more professional recording of the boys doing that song so I can shop them around to some labels. I've got a friend, Nathan. He has a recording studio here in Hollywood at his home near Mulholland Drive. He's pretty famous himself. There are a lot of his own tracks out there on a lot of songs already. Our goal for the demo will be to make sure that the boys' rendition pops."

HEADING TO HOLLYWOOD

"It's haircut time. Who's first?" I holler down the hallway. I've been cutting mine and our sons' hair since they were born—anything to save a few dollars. After a trimming and some considerable effort to get the kids dressed in their most stylish clothes, we are on our way.

The trek from San Diego to Hollywood takes about 2½ hours. Along the way, Larry and I heard enough takes of "Stop the Love" to last a lifetime.

"Guys," Larry says, still in the van. "You have every reason to be confident. This is just a recording session. Just imagine you are at home, gathered around the piano, singing your parts right on cue, and you'll nail it. Remember, these types of opportunities don't mean we have arrived or have any guarantees. During the whole process, the best you can do is trust God. He's the one who gave you your talent. He wants what's best for you, count on it."

"If you get a little nervous," I chime in, "just remember, that's the other guy talking to you. You'll do great!"

Rob pulls up, greets us, and we head up to the door.

A tall, good-looking young man with a ready smile greets us. "Hey, guys, I'm Nathan."

As they finish their introductions, he turns to Larry and me. "Sharp-looking kids. Nice manners, I like that." He turns his attention to Rob. "Hey, man, you're not gonna use this Jackson 5 song for the radio, right?"

"Nah, man," Rob clarifies. "It's just for a demo."

"OK then, let's lay this down and see what they've got."

The boys adapt well to the recording instructions as each takes a turn doing their individual parts. Within a few hours, the recording is done. Now all that remains is to mix and master the parts, which Nathan will do after we've gone.

After some small talk and sharing, we say our goodbyes.

At the car, Rob hands Larry a packet. "Go ahead and look this over. Try to get it back to me as quickly as you can."

Larry takes a brief look. "Are you OK if I have our lawyer look it over?"

"Of course. Whatever you need to do. It's pretty standard."

After Rob leaves, I turn to Larry, "We don't have a lawyer, honey."

"Yeah, I know. I'll get after it tomorrow, first thing."

While we are heading back to San Diego, Nathan is busy finessing and mastering the recording, and Rob wastes no time putting his efforts into promoting the boy band idea.

◆　◆　◆　◆

Larry takes the contract to a lawyer who has worked with Hollywood agents and artists over the years. Upon a review, he asks us to make some minor adjustments, but says it is a standard contract.

Within a few days, Rob gets back on the phone with Larry. "Hi, Larry. Any chance you could get all your guys together around the phone sometime real soon? I have something to share."

"They're all here right now, doing homework. Would this be a good time?"

"OK, guys. Is everyone there? Listen up, I've got the perfect name for you guys. *Brothers 4 Ever*, as in Brothers, the number 4, and Ever."

I loved it … got real excited and made the mistake of saying how wonderful it was before the guys got a chance to speak. As it turned out, the only one impressed with the name was Mom, and Mom didn't have enough persuasion to interest them in the name. Rob and the guys went around in circles for a while, until it became clear that Rob's mind was made up and we'd have to get used to it.

After a few minor adjustments, we sign the contract and make arrangements to go up to LA again soon to record it a second time. In all, we end up recording three times at three different studios. The responses are very positive, but not quite positive enough to guarantee getting signed by a label to produce *Brothers 4 Ever*—yet.

After about two weeks, we get a call from Rob. "Keep practicing your harmonies, work on some dance moves, and I'll keep pushing you boys to the labels. I own a magazine for teens that's big up here in Hollywood, so I have lots of connections I need to get to. Stay sharp and I'll get back to you real soon. Remember, I've got it goin' on, guys. You have talent, good looks, good voices … and being quadruplets—that's a unique hook. All you need now is publicity—as in my magazine. We're gonna get you all set up with a photo shoot. It will take place right here in the heart of Hollywood. My cousin has a limousine, and he has a friend that manages police motorcades to top it off. Get ready, because this is going to be big. I'll get back to you with the date real soon. You be ready."

31

COLLEGE-PREP EXAMS

I'm noticing this week that each of the brothers seems to exude self-confidence. They are walking with their heads held high. No doubt feeling like they are something special. Still, stardom can be elusive. It's best to stay grounded, with a solid backup plan in the interim. School deadlines are approaching, and we need to stay the course.

"Here, Mom," Brett says. He and the other boys each take turns handing me a flyer. I can't miss the bold title, "PSAT and SAT Test Prep Programs." As I read, I know it's something I'm definitely going to look into.

◆　◆　◆　◆

At the Wednesday night parents' meeting, I find myself in the company of a charming, intelligent young woman touting her company's program.

"Whatever your child gets on the first test can be improved by 100 points after completing my four-week program," she says. "The key is recognizing what your kids' weak points are and doubling up efforts with the guidance we provide. Then, when your student takes the test a second time, you'll see marked results. Sure, it's $100 to take the test again, but it's well worth it when you see that higher score, which can make a considerable difference when it comes to being accepted in the school of their choice."

That $100 per child ramps up to $400 for me in a heartbeat. Yet, I consider it to be a good gamble and will hope for the best.

After the results are in, I have a few thoughts. *Yep, she was right. Each boy's scores went up by at least 100 points. Now, all we have to do is figure out a way to afford a college education for four sons simultaneously—then help them decide which colleges they each want to apply to. Should be a breeze, if only I had a crystal ball.*

College applications are due in early January of their senior year and commitments to enroll by May 1st. *If college is where they are heading (should stardom elude them), we're going to have to start touring college campuses by their junior year. What's needed is a mechanism to help them narrow the choices of the colleges each of them want to apply to. What's that going to look like? I'd better get cracking. And I'd better be discreet about it. I'm sure no boy band manager wants to hear anything about college plans.*

It's the Packaging that Matters

Ben, Brett, Chad, and Kyle are all busy at home with school projects. Larry is at the piano in the living room plucking out parts for a four-part ensemble he wants to teach to his advanced classes at the music school. I'm sitting cross-legged at the dining room table near him, with these college brochures and financing options spread across the table.

"Honey, can I interrupt you for a moment?"

"Just give me about three minutes, OK?"

Three minutes go to five, and five turn to ten. I pick up my flute and go to our bedroom to practice my scales and arpeggios, until he hollers out that he's ready.

"OK, shoot. What's up?"

"Honey, I am so excited to share this with you. There's a program in California called the Cal Grant, and here's the deal. You are going to like this. Drumroll, please."

"Haven't we worn that one out by now?" he asks, raising his brow.

"Aw, honey, humor me. My favorite times with you are when we're silly. Just pretend you think I'm cute and fun."

Within a minute, my pom-pom and cheerleader antics have him laughing and we're both smiling.

"Here's the thing, in California, there's this grant. It's intended to help families if they have more than one child in college in any given year. I have to check about the details, but it looks to me like you pay full tuition for the first child in a California state school, and then little or no tuition at all for the other children enrolled in a Cal state school simultaneously. Can you believe it?"

"I guess we know which state our boys' college will be in," he says.

"We can narrow down the options to this: (1) Enroll in a California state school, or (2) get a full scholarship if they want to enroll in other than a Cal state school."

"Sounds like a done deal to me," he says.

"How about you keep working on your piano masterpiece for tomorrow's class. I'll make a poster to hang above the dining room table with a list of their options. I love that it gives some definition and boundaries to our dilemma."

"Good find, Janna. What a relief."

As he gets up to go back to his piano piece, I can tell that he's a little incredulous about my find. *That's OK, he'll find out it's true in due time.*

◆ ◆ ◆ ◆

Suddenly the phone rings. "Get ready," Rob says on the other end, "we're going to Hollywood. Get all the boys gathered round so they can all hear this together."

"I told you it would happen," he starts. "It's just like I said, you're gonna be bigger than some of the biggest groups you've ever heard of. We're gonna make you stars, and all the heads are going to be turning in Hollywood. Here's how it will go down. You guys and your parents will come up to Hollywood, meet with my hairstylist, and get a trim. Then we'll put you in a stretch limo with a motorcycle motorcade and drive you over to an incredibly famous clothier, where the owner will dress you to the nines. People on the streets will start looking at what's going on. You will hold your shoulders back and head high so you look real hip and sure of yourself as you walk toward your limousine. It will be waiting for you. Photographers will be there. You'll just stay cool and calm as they do their photo shoot. People will gather to see what's going on. You will look like stars, and the girls are gonna stare at you. They will figure that you are a new boy band that they just haven't heard of yet, and they'll be so excited to have gotten a chance to see you. I'll show you how it all works. Looking like a star is a big part of being a star."

◆　◆　◆　◆

As they walk out of the clothier shop in their new threads the next day, heads really do turn, watching them as they saunter up to the limousine, doors being opened for each of them. Larry and I are the last to climb in as the motorcycles warm their engines. The next stop is a very well-known record company. The producers there had heard the demo, liked what they heard, and just wanted to get a look at these four brothers on their way to stardom.

At the main office, the record company likes what they see and likes their music. All we have to do is settle on the particulars. But first, we need to wait patiently. As our guys are changing into their casual clothes for the ride home, Rob calls Larry and me aside.

"Any label we sign with will need to offer us seed money in the amount of a million dollars," he tells us. "Anything less than that indicates that the record company is not serious."

He tells us that before he met us, he had a vision that the music industry needed a new group for young teenagers, one with wholesome values and that can be a positive influence.

"When I first met the boys at Joshua Tree," he says, "it wasn't immediately obvious to me, but later it hit me—these boys are the right age, they have good morals, and their dad said they could sing. I began to think that this could be the answer to my vision. But grooming takes time. So I asked myself, *Can I do it in time for them to be released soon?* Before meeting the boys, I'd considered answering the vision by having open auditions, but I didn't look forward to all the different parents' personalities and scheduling challenges. Can you imagine organizing four singletons from four separate families? It's so much easier with this quadruplet brother's setup. I believe in these boys now, and if this record company doesn't pan out, we'll keep going until one does."

HURRY UP AND WAIT
—PLAN A OR PLAN B?

It's so confusing to be prepared for plan B when plan A is what we're all hoping for—the chance to earn a living on the big stage, making music. Every one of our sons has said they would love the opportunity to do the boy band, for a season anyway. But without exception, they all envision transitioning to one day performing their own original music, a dream we've not shared with Rob, not wanting to invite a possible conflict of visions.

◆　◆　◆　◆

We've heard nothing from Rob now for weeks. Perhaps stardom is a nonstarter for now. Still, we plan to do all we can to prepare the boys for stardom—plan A.

At the same time, we will keep the back door open with a solid readiness to step into the college track upon graduation—plan B if there are no signed offers on the table by the end of their senior year.

Defining the plan is one thing, but discerning a way to carry it out is quite another.

32

THE COLLEGE PATH

At 7:00 p.m. sharp, Ben is the first to arrive for the meeting. He stomps his foot and hollers down the stairwell into the unfinished area below that we call our basement. "Let's go, guys."

The others, who are jamming away on the drums, guitar, and trumpet, don't hear him until he calls a second time. "We're supposed to gather at the dining room table, remember?" he barks.

Getting settled, they look back and forth at Dad, and then me, and back again, both of us playing the stoic role.

"What's up?" asks Ben.

"It's a surprise," I say with half a grin.

"But we think you'll like it," says Dad.

"Remember that motorhome that was given to Mom for helping teach a middle-schooler to read?" They all nod. "Well, how would you like to grab your gear, climb into that motorhome, and drive all over California for two weeks looking at colleges?"

Kyle and Brett exchange glances. "But, Mom," says Kyle, "did you maybe forget that some mice got in it and chewed up all of the upholstery?"

"And wiring," Brett adds.

"When is spring break?" I ask, without waiting for a response. "I think you probably have a week or so to get that

RV all cleaned up, don't you? Chad and Ben, you learned a little bit about wiring when we were getting the house framed, so I think you could fix that part up." At this point, I'm trying hard not to bust out laughing. Larry gives me the nod.

"All right," I say, "let's try a changeup. How would you like it if we rent a brand-new 31-foot motorhome with bunks for everybody and do the college tour that way?"

Hoots, hollers, jumping up and down, and lots of bear hugs accompany my announcement.

We pass out full-color brochures to each of them that show the gleaming new motorhome. I bask in the joy of their exuberance as they start scheming on what they'll want to bring along with them on our grand adventure.

As I contact the various schools, I play up the multiples thing, managing to arrange cafeteria sampling for most, tours for several, and an overnight in the dorms for a couple of the schools. Excitement is growing exponentially.

PLAN B SET IN MOTION

It's April 4, 1998, the Saturday before Palm Sunday, and we're on our way toward our first stop. The motorhome is loaded with musical instruments, skateboards, rollerblades, golf clubs, tennis rackets, balls of all sorts, and even our dog, Dusty. The six bikes strapped to the back of the rig assures us that the brothers will be able to zip around and through each campus to get an up-close and personal read on each of the seventeen prospects they have settled on visiting.

After two full weeks of college-hopping, each of our guys has a much better picture of what college life is like and has zeroed in on his first, second, and third schools of choice. Now they are better equipped to home in on the final stretch. Each young man will know which colleges have accepted him within six months.

LIFE GOES ON

"I wouldn't look in that car or open that trunk if I were you. That's right, I'm watching you, Chad," I say with a wink.

"Why? What's going on?"

"It's a surprise."

As Dad piles the kids into the car, I say, "Give me a 30-minute warning before you head home."

◆　◆　◆　◆

What I couldn't find at Home Depot, I found at the Army Surplus store: heavy 12-gauge 60-foot extension cords, shop lights, heavy-duty staple gun, area rugs, and tarps in the boys' favorite colors.

With the family gone, I'm able to launch my unconventional project without having to justify any of the steps along the way.

Five hours of working alone in the basement take their toll. Setting down my tools on the newly laid concrete floor, I give in to exhaustion. Collapsing on to one of the plush new color-coordinated rugs beside me, I drift into a deep sleep.

As my body recharges, my dreams take me all the way back to those days at the beach, the boys three years old, making sandcastles at the shore in La Jolla until it was time for them to have their naps, each on his own beach towel. With them fast asleep, we often reminisced about our life together up to then, imagining what kind of men our sons would grow to be. The dream scene changes. There is only me on the sand. Larry and his 16-year-old sons are on their surfboards or boogie boards. I've dug my toes into the cool sand, falling asleep to the rhythm of the waves and the calling of the gulls flying above me. I'm startled by the wave that comes clear up to my chin, quickly cooling me. Sensing danger, I wake up. Dusty is licking my face, alerting me to something. I realize that the phone is ringing. I grab it just in time. Larry asks if the guys can pick up hot fudge sundae supplies on the way home, giving me just enough time to get everything in order for the big unveiling.

A little while later, like clockwork, Dusty lets me know that the guys are just about here with his traditional two barks, followed by his full throttle sprint up the driveway a few feet ahead of the five of them in the Pontiac 5000, with Dad at the wheel.

The door flies open as they rush in, anxious to tell me about their time with Dad.

"Hold on, hold on. You're going to want to see this before it gets dark," I say.

"See what," Ben asks.

"Get the ice cream in the freezer. Then go down the stairwell, open the door, and find your new room."

He looks at me suspiciously.

"It's unconventional, but it's yours and I think you'll have fun with it."

"Mom," Brett says, "do we each have a bedroom downstairs?"

"Yep, that's exactly what I'm saying. You can get settled in as soon as Dad helps you take apart the bunk beds and get them down there. You each have a long extension cord, so electricity will go to each of the rooms. The walls are really easy to change if you ever want to change them, since they're just made out of painted tarps attached to the ceiling joists. Go on down there. Find the one that's your color, and that will be your room."

Larry just stands there, stunned. He looks at the boys and then back at me, no doubt wondering if this is going to fly. It does. The 1800 square foot unfinished basement is put to good use. It becomes the cool place of the neighborhood to make music in and just hang out in, with plenty of room to spare. Now the upstairs bedrooms are up for grabs. Larry gets the office he's longed for, and I'll eke out a guest room. We'll finish the basement in stages—someday. This is as much closure as I've felt in a long time, and it's glorious.

MAY 1999—SUSPENSE

Tiptoeing down the stairs at 1:00 a.m., I pause, not wanting to interrupt the sleep of my sons.

This is the season of torture, waiting and wondering, fighting to keep my wits about me, as we all wait for the results of the twenty college admission applications we sent out to the institutions we thought most viable. I check the mailbox daily before the guys get home from school. Nothing yet.

What if all but one gets accepted? What if colleges steer clear of multiples? What if they entertain the idea of enrolling multiples but are especially fascinated by the identicals, entertaining some sort of twisted hope that Ben and Chad could be used as study specimens in the psychology department of their school? What if one of the four of them gets multiple acceptances and is tempted to lord it over his brothers? What if the elusive boy band finally launches and college is a moot point?

What if? What if? What if?

Dusty walks lightly down the steps to where I've paused. Perhaps he senses that this is a poignant moment for me. He nuzzles up, licking my cheeks, then looks up.

"I'm going to need your love, old boy. Let's go in and see how our boys are doing."

Opening the door quietly, I walk in with Dusty right behind me. Grabbing a pillow, I sit down on the floor in the middle of the now recently framed and finished four-bedroom, two-bath basement.

"OK, buddy, you know the routine." And I do what I've done time and again in pivotal seasons, from their infancy all the way to this present moment. I close my eyes and listen to them breathing. It calms me. My anxiety eventually gives way to hope and peace. Praying for each child by name, I'm finally free to let go of my control, as I release Ben, Brett, Chad, and Kyle into God's perfect care once again.

33

THE RESULTS ARE IN

Kyle had planned on attending UCSD in San Diego. But after much deliberation, he settles on Cal Poly at San Luis Obispo on the central coast of California. The setting is a small, idyllic, agricultural town with lots of activities and adventures within walking or bike-riding distance. It includes a downtown farmer's market event every Thursday evening with food, games, and plenty of live music. The dorms on campus are in a kind of pod-like setting, each pod having several dorm rooms clustered around a central shared living area, which includes a small kitchen, conducive to making new friends and connections.

The hands-on, learn-by-doing style appeals to him, although he says he has a bit of a dilemma about being the only one in the family to choose a school that isn't near home. He's ruminating over the question of *What do I want to do?* compared to *What are my brothers doing?* He says that maybe this will be an opportunity to develop independence. Plus, he says he might have an opportunity to walk onto a sports team as a singleton for once.

In the end, he says the deal-maker comes down to this: "Do I like the culture of this place? Am I going to fit in here? Will I be able to make friends? Is the food good in the cafeteria? And hey, is there a golf course nearby?"

And I'm thinking, *We as the parents can't be anything but thrilled, because he has decided to be a history major —and we all know that gives you a real good chance of getting a job upon graduation.* I laugh to myself and take comfort in remembering that I changed my major numerous times at SDSU, and yet things seemed to have worked out pretty well. Lots of unknowns, but lots of opportunities.

Chad says he doesn't want to go to the same school as Ben because "I want my independence and I want people to know my name." He decides on Point Loma Nazarene University, right on the cliffs above the Pacific Ocean in the San Diego area. It's an awesome setting with a low student-to-instructor ratio, with some of the upper-level classes having as few as five to six students with a professor. He will be even closer to his passion for surfing daily. He has a brilliant math mind and is focused on mathematics and computer science. The food in the cafeteria is catered by the Marriott Hotel, so no complaints there! To top it off, he has been awarded almost a full scholarship, which will make this rather pricey private school an option for him.

So, he figures he will be known as "Just Chad," without the confusion of "Are you Chad or Ben?" When he tells me this, he does so with a wink and a smile.

That seemed like no problem, as Ben was dead set on Westmont College, a small private Christian liberal arts college, located in scenic Santa Barbara with views of the hills and ocean below. He was accepted and all systems were go. Also, Ben said, "I want to be known as Ben, not just one of the quads."

But now there's a hiccup along that path. With Chad receiving a significant scholarship, Ben wonders if he might be able to get one as well. After applying to Point Loma, he too is accepted on a scholarship. He chooses Industrial Psychology as his major, an area at first beyond my scope of understanding.

So there it is, the Ben/Chad, Chad/Ben, "Which one are you?" conundrum continues. At least they won't be staying in the same dorm. Chad's desire to be known as "Just Chad" is put on hold.

Brett has a different take on things altogether. In his own words, "I loved the college tour, Mom, because I wanted to explore California and find as many good skating spots as possible. I'm just not ready to be a grown-up. I have all the social skills but absolutely NO direction. I don't want to go to college. Not yet anyway."

Stunned, I go numb, wondering where and when this change in direction took place. *How could I have missed it?*

On Friday, I'll take a personal day and head to the SDSU counseling center to meet with an enrollment advisor. Hopefully, she'll listen to my dilemma as we talk through the possible outcomes of the options in front of us.

◆　◆　◆　◆

"I don't envy you on this one," the counselor admits. "I mean, it's enough to have quadruplets in the first place, but then to have to work through something like this—it's got to be gut wrenching."

I nod.

"The best I can do is let you know the statistical probabilities of going to college after taking a year off following high school. They're not pretty. Perhaps you could strike a deal with Brett."

"Go on, I'm listening."

"Maybe he can be persuaded to attend college for an agreed-upon length of time, say one year, and then be given the option to continue or not. At least that way he won't have to wrestle later with that demon that tickles his mind saying that he missed his chance. That's what I would do if he were my son."

In the end, I have a few things to discuss and mull over with Larry when we sit down together this evening.

◆　◆　◆　◆

"So what do you think of all of that, honey," I ask following a brief rundown.

"I'm with you."

Brett decides to follow our advice and attend San Diego State University as a music major, with trumpet his primary instrument. He will be near home, friends, and musical con-nections, but most importantly, a plethora of skate parks and rails to explore.

"OK, Mom and Dad, I'm agreeing to give it a try for one year. That on-campus connections thing looks pretty good."

At peace with his decision, he continues. "It looks like there's a lot of rails I can use to skate on there too."

"Oh yeah, like I'm really happy about that," I say, as I tilt my head back and roll my eyes.

"Don't worry, Mom, I promise I'll wear my helmet." He pats me on the back, pulling me into a reassuring bear hug.

THE DREADED CALL

I look anxiously at the phone every time it rings. The boy band drama is either in hibernation or completely dead, which fills me simultaneously with disappointment and relief.

Getting up from the piano bench, Larry opens the door and heads into the kitchen for a refill on his coffee.

"So, my wonderful husband," I say as I fill his cup and hand him a muffin. "Have you decided what to do about that phone call?"

"Phone call?"

"Yeah, the one you're going to make to their manager about the graduation party."

"I'm pretty much dreading that call, you know," he says.

"I don't blame you, but we at least have to let him know what direction our family is going in. We can't just leave him hanging. How about you gather your thoughts, and when you're ready, I'll make myself scarce in the other room, praying for a peaceful outcome."

"OK, I guess it's unavoidable."

Twenty minutes later, Larry bounces back into the room. He's a good actor, but not this time.

"Was it that bad?"

"No, it was worse. Rob was, of course, unaware that we have our college plan B waiting in the wings. I don't think he saw that coming. He listened to me for a few minutes as I told him about the guys getting accepted to various colleges—planning to move on campus in just two months. I assured him that we would keep the possibility open for a boy band, but that we have to move forward in the meantime with plans for attending college. If the boy band opportunities are a ways off, the acceptance period would have passed us by while waiting."

"I'd venture that it was a pretty hard blow for him to take."

"He was quite emphatic about insisting that they wouldn't be going to college because there are so many deals in the works. He ended with, 'You just be ready for my phone call,' and his tone was insistent."

"I guess that means he won't be coming to the high school graduation party?"

We laugh.

"Let's take a walk and shake it off," I say. "You did the right thing, babe, and it took a lot of guts."

GRADUATION, SPRING 1999

"You survived the ceremony," Larry says reassuringly. "Are you up for the graduation party? Are you going to be able to do this?"

"Just watch me. I'm all geared up for this part," I say.

He looks at me doubtfully.

"All right, I do have a bunch of tissues stashed in my purse just in case."

The casual barn-style high school hangout is packed to capacity with family, church friends, and more than a few adoring teenage girls, many of them hanging out around the pool table, watching their favorite Wagner boy and dancing to the music cranked up high on the CD player.

I stop to watch as one brave girl steps up to the pool table and clears it.

I'm thinking, *You go, girl. Keep them humble.*

My sons are intoxicated with the freedom to throw back soda after soda—for once without limits. They look happy with the volume of food and drinks at their fingertips.

Their hair is neat and tidy. Each son looks like he's ready for a successful future, beginning with their first year of college in the fall.

"OK, everyone," Larry announces into the mic at the front of the room. "Janna and I would like everyone to get settled so that we can join together to give these young men a classy send-off."

Facing his sons, he continues. "Sons, would you come to the right side of the platform and sit in these four chairs while we all watch a slideshow of the high points in your life to date?"

Without hesitation, they all scramble to their seat on the platform.

Ten minutes into the slideshow I peek into the audience, wondering if it's just all too much. Larry's younger brother, Jon, is busting up laughing, and it's contagious. I drop my shoulders and enjoy the show.

At last, Larry and I come to the front, gathering the boys around us, our arms over their shoulders. We deliver a handful of poignant words of congratulations and I make good use of the tissues in my pocket.

"Now it's your turn, friends," I say, as I hold the mic in the air. "You can make sweet sincere comments, or even give them a roast if you're in the mood. They can take it. Who will be first?"

Then it backfires. After a few people share, Brett grabs the mic, turns to look at Larry and me, and delivers a heart-wrenching but greatly exaggerated soliloquy of what wonderful parents we are.

Awkward. Are they really compelled to say these things? Or could this be the Wagner competition influencing their actions? I ask myself.

Now I find myself in that awkward position of "I didn't see that coming." Reaching deep inside, I struggle, looking for a way to recover. Then I chuckle, remembering 1981 when the news interviewer was looking down at Larry holding Kyle, then five months old. Larry was bouncing Kyle wildly on his knee while being interviewed. The newscaster asked, "How do you manage with four?"

At that very moment, Kyle threw up with a jet-propelled blast across the living-room floor. Larry looked up, his hand reached over, systematically grabbing a barf rag, and said, "And that's how you manage quadruplets—plenty of rags."

That memory lightens my mood. *Just recover and continue. What else can you do?*

As planned, we wrap up the event with a declaration of autonomy. With all of our guests seated, we ask Ben, Brett, Chad, and Kyle to stand and face us.

With all of our guests as witnesses, Larry and I declare together, "1, 2, 3 … we set you free."

34

TRANSITIONS

Dusty is curled up at my feet in my quilting cubby as I put the finishing touches on the fourth quilt I've created since our sons left home. As he nestles in to lick my feet, I look down and scratch the nape of his neck.

"Dusty, old friend, your loyalty soothes my aching heart. I'm not sure I'd make it through this without you."

Hearing the crunch of the gravel at the bottom of the driveway, he jumps up to push open the screen door.

"I'm home," Larry calls out as he sets down his briefcase on the entry bench. "Where are you, babe?"

"Right here in my cubby, but I'm just about ready to finish dinner. You hungry?"

"No hurry. What are you up to in there?"

"Just finishing another quilt."

"Oh, that looks good." He hesitates as he eyeballs the quilt. "Gee, isn't that a little bit feminine for a guy?"

"Yeah, it is, but I'm making it for a girl."

"A girl? What girl?"

"No girl in particular. I'll just donate it to the quilt shop. They'll know someone who needs a little bit of encouragement, and I'm enjoying doing something girly. I'm calling it my 'empty-nest therapy.' I'll tell you all about it. Probably more than you ever wanted to know. So, you ready to eat?" I close the folding door of my quilt cubby, and Larry opens his arms for a hug.

As we're cleaning up the kitchen together after dinner he asks, "So, honey, with that project you've got going, is your sadness going away?"

"Not a chance, but it helps take the edge off. I'm really glad that I'm busy all day long with students and then grading papers. But on these four nights a week when your classes don't finish until long after dark, I find that I torture myself—going downstairs, walking from one empty room to the other, and wondering what our sons are doing, what they're thinking, how their outlooks might be changing. It's a rite of passage, I know, but I don't have to pretend I like it."

"Dang, honey, that must be tough. I admit that I don't quite get it, but I sure do hate to see you hurting like that. Hey, here's something to perk you up."

I tilt my head to my shoulder and look up at him. "What's that?"

"Thanksgiving isn't that far away, and they'll all be here for the break."

"Yeah, and I'm glad. But I'm also bracing myself, wanting to be gracious when they want to spend time with their friends."

"Trust me, honey, I'll make sure they spend time with you."

"That's the thing, I don't want to lay a guilt trip on them. They need to live their lives and I need to adapt to the situation. You seem to be doing just fine with it yourself."

"Yeah, I kind of like it," he says with a smile.

"I'll come around in time, you'll see."

After One Year of College —'Plan A' Comes to Visit

It's May, and the boys are home for the summer. They are chowing down a rather large hamburger lunch.

"How does it feel to have a year of school under your belt?" I ask.

"I'm glad we decided to do college," Ben says.

"Me too," says Kyle.

"Any word from Rob?"

"No, we're figuring it's done," I say.

"I'll bet you're disappointed, Brett," Larry chides.

"Ha, ha, Dad. Not. Even though I broke my ankle skating and pulled out of school for a while, I am loving my freedom."

"We know you guys have your own plans for today. Maybe we'll see you for dinner?" Larry asks.

"Go ahead and do your thing. I can have dinner ready at 7:00," I say. "Would that work?"

They all agree.

Just as Larry and I settle into some couple time, the phone rings. It's Rob. It seems we are to be thrust back into a full-on plan A, beginning as soon as June. The boy band is still alive.

"I don't know if that's a good or bad thing from the kids' point of view," I say.

"Well, all we can do is lay it out there and check their responses," Larry says.

"Yeah, but a gig with the San Diego Padres should get their attention for sure."

◆　◆　◆　◆

At dinner, I ask, "Does everyone still like baseball?"

They nod.

"Do you especially like your home team, the Padres?"

"What are you getting at, Mom?"

"Would you like to go to their sky show game on June 16th?" Larry asks.

"Really?" Kyle asks.

"You're going to get all of that and more," I say.

"What do you mean?" Chad asks.

"Rob called today," Larry says. "It's been requested that you sing the national anthem a cappella in four-part harmony to open the game, ending with a jet flyover."

"So Brothers 4 Ever will get a lot of recognition," I say.

They all burst into cheers of excitement. As it begins to die down and they ask for more of the particulars, Kyle speaks up.

"We'll get to watch the game, right?"

"I would certainly think so," I say.

"We should start working on your harmonies right after dinner," Larry says.

Brothers 4 Ever is in full gear again.

◆　◆　◆　◆

It's June 16, 2000, before the Padres game. The boys' interview with ABC News is an all-day event, with coverage beginning at the house. Herb Cawthorne and his cameraman are hanging out to capture all the excitement for the newscast tonight. It becomes obvious that Rob wasted no time getting the boys a gig to air on national television.

Trevor Hoffman and Tony Gwynn will be there, as the Padres play the Reds. This is the long-awaited last game at the Jack Murphy/Qualcomm Stadium before the team moves their home games downtown to Petco Park. The stands will be packed. Add to that the anticipation of the annual sky show, and it's not surprising that it takes a police escort to get our guys to their check-in point, past all the traffic backed up for a half mile.

Larry and I are ushered from the limo to our seats in the stands where we will be able to watch our sons walk out to the field to sing the national anthem, a cappella. Anticipation grows as the Padres girls move toward the limo to escort the foursome to the edge of the field, in the same order they will be in as they walk to the pitcher's mound.

The sound engineer makes his way over, gathers them in a circle, handing each of them an earplug. He explains that there is a full one-second delay, a latency, between their voices and the voice the fans will hear in the stands.

"You should be sure your earplug is pushed in tight and lean in toward each other so that you hear mostly your voices and not the ones that are being projected into the stands. It's tricky and takes a lot of concentration. Best if you focus on listening to each other and block out all the other echoes and sounds. You got that?"

They nod and turn toward the Padres girls, indicating that they are ready to go. With heads up and shoulders back, they look dignified and friendly all at once as they walk single file to their mark, where they will sing for an excited group of fans.

First in is Kyle, who will sing the melody part, followed by Ben, singing the bassline. Next comes Brett, who will sing the tenor part, and Chad will bring up the rear, singing baritone.

"Please stand for the national anthem," the announcer says, "to be led by Brothers 4 Ever—Ben, Brett, Chad, and Kyle Wagner." All 69,000 souls stand, and the players take off their hats. Brett sounds the tuning note on his handheld pitch pipe. They continue humming the pitch above the roar of the crowd until Brett raises his head. They all take a deep breath and begin in sync on his cue—fully engaged in the task at hand, doing what they love to do, sing for an audience.

The fireworks go off on cue, as the boys sing "and the rockets' red glare …"

The atmosphere explodes with excitement as our foursome sings "O'er the land of the free, and the home of the brave." Just as they punch the last note in four-part harmony, the jets fly over, followed by the boom of their engines.

As the players take their positions on the field, the Brothers 4 Ever are ushered back by the Padres girls.

My eyes moisten in pride as I take it all in, wondering if they'll get a chance to meet a baseball player, Kyle's number-one goal for the day, being the sports fan that he is.

They begin to walk up to the seats by us but are quickly told by their manager that it would be unprofessional to hang out with the fans. I watch them as they continue walking up to their reserved seats anyway.

As the first inning is getting underway, I notice that our sons are not even glancing at the many people turning their heads to get a look at them.

Are they really that oblivious to the onlookers? They seem equally oblivious to the gesturing of their manager, who clearly wants them out of the stands.

When the fans stand up to applaud the opening play, Rob seizes the opportunity to get their attention. He scampers up into the stands and tells us that the limo driver needs to get going.

Reluctantly, they acquiesce.

I smile to myself, delighted to see that they're not so caught up in wanting to be stars that they can't grasp the opportunity to behave like everyday teenagers.

The full motorcade and stretch limo usher us back to our rural home in Jamul, some twenty miles to the southeast of the stadium.

As the guys climb out, probably anxious to change into their everyday clothes, the manager stops them in their tracks.

"Not so fast, guys. Remember what you've got coming up in just three weeks?" They pause. He continues. "You've gotten to record with Jamie Jones at his studio in Hollywood. He told you that you have a lot of potential. He has lots of connections. Those songs you recorded with him got you into Sony Records, which, by the way, wants you to do the showcase in three weeks so they can have a look-see at your progress. They are going to be sending out scouts, so this may be the break we've been looking for. In fact, reps from Quincy Jones have also said they'd be there, along with several other labels."

"Hey, Rob," Brett says cautiously. "We have our birthday coming up on July 6th and then we'll start college again soon after that. I think I speak for all of us when I say that we'll probably want to spend a little time with family and friends before the showcase."

"OK, Brett, you do that. But at the same time, ask yourself this: Will you be having other birthdays and fun times in the future?"

Chad chimes in, "Well, of course."

"Then answer this: Do you think you're going to have very many opportunities to be in a showcase like the one coming up, complete with national attention, recording companies and all, reps from record labels, wondering if they should sign you guys?"

Silence.

He continues. "Yeah, that's what I thought. So, grab this opportunity and do everything you can to improve the odds. I'll send a choreographer down here real soon. You do your own part in the meantime … practice your vocal parts, come up with some of your own dance moves."

He turns to me. "Weren't you a dance major for a while in college, Janna?" (I nod.)

He turns to the boys. "Well then, you guys listen to what your mom says and see what you can put together. As for going back to college, I don't even wanna hear that kind of talk. You won't be going back to college—you'll be too busy making records and making money."

THREE WEEKS LATER—SHOWTIME

"What do you think?" I ask Larry. "Are we gonna be able to cram all of our gear into the van with the six of us?"

"We'll have to make it work. The studio is responsible for all the electronics, amps, mikes, lighting, the whole deal. We'll need to be sure the guys load up their two guitars and saxophone. But that's it. There will be a piano set up on the stage already. It's a standard concert setup."

◆　◆　◆　◆

"Oh, shoot, we're going to want to avoid the rush-hour traffic to LA, aren't we?"

"Too late for that now," Larry says.

Walking down the steep narrow hallway to the basement, I hear the cacophony of hubbub even before I open the door. Clothes are strewn across the room. Ben is at the piano, Brett and Chad have guitars, and Kyle is playing the keys as they practice.

"Shouldn't you be packing it up right about now?"

"Mom," Chad says. "We need to show them that we're versatile. We don't want to be a band that just plays with the tracks. We want to be able to play some original songs and play our instruments too. So this is our chance to prove that we can do it. We have to get it right. Just one more time through, OK, Mom?"

"All right, how about I listen to you play it one more time, then let's get cracking."

When they finish, they gather up their gear and throw it in the van.

"Mom, have you and Dad heard anything about a choreographer meeting us at the hotel?" Ben asks.

"No, not yet. Dad and I think you'll probably just have to do it the Wagner way."

"What's the Wagner way?"

"We pull it together as a family, trusting that someone up above is watching out for us."

"So, three days at the hotel to figure out our own choreography, and then the showcase?" Kyle asks.

I nod.

"No problem, guys," he says, his voice filled with confidence. "I've got a lot of ideas. We can do this."

With Chad, Ben, Kyle, and Brett brainstorming together in the back seat, Larry and I take time to talk.

◆　　◆　　◆　　◆

THE ABC EYEWITNESS NEWS STORY

"In music news, there's a new boy band ready to take America by storm. But this one is different. The four teenagers are not only brothers—they are quadruplets, and they're out to get a record deal. Meet Kyle, Ben, Chad, and Brett—*Brothers 4 Ever.*"

[Quick shot of the boys singing the main line of "Stop Runnin' from Love," on stage with dance moves]

The anchor continues:

"From the suburbs of San Diego, this quadruplet quartet of 19-year-olds call themselves *Brothers 4 Ever.* Their goal …?"

Ben speaks into the News-7 microphone, "A group with a lot of talent that knows how to entertain, that knows how to play from their hearts, and whatever they feel like playing, they're going to play."

[A quick shot of the boys singing the national anthem, a cappella, on stage]

The anchor continues: "The brothers plan to maintain a clean, wholesome image."

[Quick shot of the boys singing the main line of "Everything You Want"]

The anchor continues:

"The brothers also have a strong faith in God, and if they hit it big, His Word might become part of their music."

This time, Brett speaks into the mic. "If millions of people around the world are buying our stuff, and there's a couple of songs about God in there, then I think that will definitely be good."

Chad gets his turn with the interviewer, "The goal, in the long run, is not the fortune and the fame, and the girls, and ya know, getting everything we want. It's the spread of a good message to everybody …"

"We're kinda tryin' to stand out from the other boy bands," Kyle says. "First of all, our music is different—it's kind of a mixture of everything—and we want to send a good message."

"*Brothers 4 Ever* made their LA debut last night for the record industry, and several labels showed up to hear them."

35

THE WAIT

Our family is at home now, at peace with their performance, and exhilarated with the response of the media. The atmosphere was abuzz with possibility thinking throughout the three-hour drive home to San Diego County.

"You guys go ahead and get some sleep now," Larry says. "We'll take care of all the stuff tomorrow."

"But what do you think, Mom and Dad? Do you think we'll hear from anybody as soon as tomorrow maybe?"

"Maybe," Dad says, "but not likely. The music label reps will need to talk to their higher-ups and decide if they feel like there's enough potential there."

"But what do you guys think?" Chad asks. "I mean, do you think we did a good enough job at it to catch their eye and their ear?"

I speak up. "Watching from the ready room as you guys performed, I forced myself to look at the audience to see how they reacted."

"Yeah, and what did you think?"

"I saw a lot of smiles and nods, even some shared glances back and forth from a couple of reps from Sony."

"And? Tell us more. What did you think? What were they saying? Did they like us?"

"I'm pretty sure everyone liked you, as you are likable guys."

Brett butts in. "Come on, Mom, don't just tell us what we want to hear."

"All right then. I had expected to see more enthusiasm and was disappointed for a minute. Then I realized that these are reps from different companies. If they like what they see, they will end up competing against each other for representation. So it seems pretty reasonable to me that they would make an effort to hide their emotions. Does that make sense to you?"

"Yeah, I get that," Brett says with a sigh. "But it's just so frustrating not to know."

"It's torture for all of us," Larry says, as he reaches over to squeeze my hand.

"So what can we do about it, guys?" I ask.

It goes quiet for a few seconds.

"Keep practicing?" Kyle asks.

"Focus on getting ready for college again, in case we don't get signed?" Ben chimes in.

"Take time to connect with old friends?" Chad asks.

"All wonderful suggestions—spot-on," I say. "And there's one more—the most important thing. You know what I'm talking about?" I ask.

"Pray," they all say at once.

"Sometimes the best thing you can do to take control of the situation is to let go of the outcome."

Waking up to some shuffling around in the kitchen the next morning, I saunter out to find Ben, dressed in his running shoes and T-shirt, eating cold cereal and watching TV.

"Morning, Ben. Headed out for a run this morning?"

"Oh, hi, Mom. Didn't know you were up."

"Yeah, it felt great just to sleep in a bit. How long will your run be today?" I ask.

"I'm aiming for seven miles."

I smile, shaking my head. "I don't get how you can do that."

"It feels pretty good when I hit that zone and I just keep on running until I reach my goal. The day goes best for me when I start with a run."

"What about your bros, do you know what they're up to?"

"I heard Brett and Chad talking about doing some extreme skating. I suppose they'll probably meet up with some of their friends and try to find some good rails to skate."

"Nothing like good old fear to send the mama bear to her knees praying for their safety," I say. "And Kyle?"

"He said last night that he wants to get together with some of the guys from his high school tennis team. They're still in town for the summer."

"Sounds great. You kids finally have a chance to just chill and be spontaneous for a few days."

"Kids?" Ben says. "We're nineteen now, Mom. We don't really think of ourselves as kids anymore."

"Oh, yeah, that's right." I pause. "It's weird," I say.

"Weird? Why is that?"

"Yeah, I suppose 'kids' isn't quite right … but 'sons' sounds formal and 'men' doesn't roll off my tongue very easily. Is it still OK if I refer to you as *the guys*?"

"Yeah, that works," he says as he walks out from behind the family room sofa to give me a hug.

The next few days fly by as I make desperate attempts to slow the pace of the hourglass measuring out the time left for me to be with my guys.

◆　◆　◆　◆

With two days remaining before college resumes, the phone rings at 2:00 p.m. Larry is at the music school and the guys have all left the house for the day. As I scurry up the stairs trying to get to the phone in the kitchen before the sixth ring, I wonder if maybe the agent is finally calling.

"Hello," I say with an optimistic lilt in my voice.

"Hey, babe," Larry says. "I've gotta make this quick. I have a class starting in a couple of minutes."

"Oh, sure. Did you hear from Rob?"

"No, not yet, but maybe I will before I get home. Dunno. I did hear from Brett. He says he wants us all to have a sit-down tonight as a family. I figure the boys have some questions about where to go from here, what Rob's been saying, and all that. Can we plan for a family meeting at, say, 7:00 tonight?"

"Sure, I'll throw together a quick dinner that everyone can just grab when they're ready."

"Great. I've gotta go, but I'll see you real soon. Love you."

"I love you more." Click.

◆　◆　◆　◆

As we are all waiting for Dad to get home, the kids have gathered downstairs. They have the door closed, and it's odd, but they are talking in low tones. They did close the door, and I will respect their boundary in keeping with my newfound determination to let go.

In a few minutes, Ben comes up and asks if they can eat their pizza downstairs.

Trying to hide my disappointment, I say, "Sure, here ya go."

When he reaches the bottom of the stairs, he closes the door and it goes quiet—oddly quiet. They are talking in muffled tones.

◆　◆　◆　◆

When Larry gets home, he sets down his briefcase in the entry, takes me in his arms for a big hug, hollering out over his shoulder, "I'm home, guys."

Kyle hollers back from the basement, "We'll be up there in a few minutes, Dad."

"What's that all about?" Larry asks me.

"I wish I knew. They've been talking quietly down there for almost an hour now."

As Larry grabs his pizza and chows down, he says, "I heard from Rob."

Just then, one by one they come up the stairs, not bounding up as is the norm. They seem more sedate, less competitive as they slowly walk up—first Ben, then Chad, Kyle, and finally Brett.

Larry gives me a look and says, "I'll tell you all at once."

As we all settle in the living room, I notice that the atmosphere is decidedly different tonight. But my jovial, fun-loving husband pays no heed, initiating a bit of lighthearted rough-housing. It seems to me to be received awkwardly by our sons. But I reason that they are perhaps uneasy about the increasingly unknown direction their lives will be taking within the next couple of days.

"I heard from Rob today," Larry says, expecting an excited response. It falls flat.

"We're still going to keep trying," he continues. "But Rob says that the record labels all agree you need more preening. He says that after we have a little more to show in the way of choreography, they will be very interested in looking at you again."

We are taken aback when one by one by one our sons each speak their mind about discontinuing this boy band idea in favor of finishing college. Each of them agrees that this is the only time they can enjoy a college education as a young person.

"Look, boys, I know how you feel," Larry says, "but this could take more time and patience than we expected. We've come this far. Wouldn't it be nice to be successful as a boy band for a few years, rack up millions of dollars in the bank, and then go to college? You'd be financially independent."

"Dad," Ben says, "we've given this thing a good three years, almost four, and we've attended college for a year already. This Hollywood thing may or may not ever go, but one thing's for sure—we have the opportunity to go to college, and that's a sure deal."

"Besides, Dad," Brett says, "our style is morphing into something decidedly different from what Rob wants us to do. We'd like to be able to play our own instruments and come up with our own music. It seems that the boy band music is being covered very well by groups like NSYNC and others."

"I could go either way," says Kyle, "but it doesn't seem like we're really getting anywhere with it."

"Well, Kyle," says Chad, "you and Brett pretty much have all the solos, and that's okay, but as for me, I want to be able to play guitar. That's my passion. And as far as trusting that we're going to get famous and make millions of dollars, I think you just have to look at the track record."

"Well," Dad says, "you did an original song at the show-case, but they want to see NSYNC-type stuff. That's what's hot these days."

As I look at Larry, I sense the weight of disappointment falling onto his shoulders. He turns to me.

"Do you want to have a go at convincing them to keep trying?" he asks.

Silence follows as my head drops down and my eyes close. My mind takes me back to their high school days. Scenes of house building, beach camping, sporting events, roughhous-ing, and music-making flash before me, finally coming to rest on the vision of their high school graduation party.

I see them walking amongst their friends, family members, former teachers, and pastors, hearts full of hope for the future in front of them.

The scene changes and I see my own self in the vision, holding Larry's hand and declaring in unison with him, "1, 2, 3, we set you free."

The haziness of the scene begins to clear.

"Mom?"

"Janna?"

"Mom, are you OK?"

I lift my chin and open my eyes.

"Oh, yes. I'm content. Exquisitely so."

They look at me—Brett, Ben, Chad, Kyle, and Larry, all looking puzzled. I lean my head to the left, reach out for both of Larry's hands, and hold them tightly in clear sight of our sons.

"Do you remember, darling, the graduation party?"

He nods, and I pause.

"We concluded the party with our declaration, '1, 2, 3, we set you free.'"

The corners of his lips begin to curl up, perhaps because he senses what's coming next.

"We set them free a year ago and promised to support them in their endeavors. We declared to them and ourselves that they were adults."

"I guess it's really not our decision, is it, Jan?"

"No, it's not, and we need to let go and support them."

"I hate it when you're so obviously right," he says with a chuckle, lightening the tension.

"Group hug?" I ask.

"Sure, let's do it," Larry says.

We all wrap our arms around each other. My eyes mist a bit and I reach out for a tissue. The air seems to get decidedly light around us.

A new and unexpected emotion wraps its arms around me. What is that? It feels foreign to me.

Then I realize in an instant, this is what closure feels like. And I like it.

EPILOGUE

Some years later, with our sons well established on their individual career paths, I am basking in the freedom of frequent spontaneity.

I am a math teacher at Monta Vista High School in east San Diego County. I have just enough responsibility to keep the loneliness of an empty nest at bay. Larry devotes himself to the development of Wagner's School of Music.

Our favorite jam is tennis; we jokingly refer to ourselves as tennis addicts. I join my husband in one of those ever-so-fun, spring tennis club, mixed doubles tournaments in the desert.

Larry is a strong player and very steady, so he can deliver warm-up balls to me one after the other with fairly good accuracy and at reasonable speeds. We determine to get up early and start warming up at 7:00 a.m. before any of the other players arrive. This allows me time for a solid warm-up, which always boosts my confidence.

And then it happens. As I reach out to hit the ball, my toe catches on a flaw in the court's pavement, sending me through the air as I try to regain my balance.

I hit my shoulder and head hard, and people come running from courts across the way to see what is going on.

"What was that big thud?"

"What's wrong? Are you OK? Should we call an ambulance?"

I touch Larry's hip and look at him, shaking my head with a gentle "No, I feel fine. There's no blood. Let's not make a thing of this. I'm fine. Really, I'm just fine."

So, we begin the tournament, score well, and everything seems dandy. We go home and get back into our daily routines as if nothing had happened. I push the memory of the percussive *boom* to the back of my mind.

But everything was not OK. At first, there were subtle changes that became more obvious as time passed. It became harder and harder for me to teach with confidence. I was nervous and vulnerable.

I recognized that I was slipping mentally. The words on the page were harder and harder to read. Yet, when I went in for my optometry checkups, no changes were perceived in my vision.

"You're actually nearly 20/20 in your vision and probably only need a little correction for reading," I was told. But how could that be? I was now barely able to make out words on a page.

In complete denial, I keep things to myself and rationalize that it's all part of the natural aging process.

At first, I can believe that, but as time passes, I begin to think, "Oh no, it could be Alzheimer's." I'm afraid to get tested, afraid of what I might hear. I pray. I agonize, fearful of the unknown.

One day at the front of my seventh period, ninth grade algebra/geometry/trigonometry class, I'm going over an equation on the whiteboard with the kids. All is going fine until one of the students says, "Mrs. Wagner, you could do it another way also."

He begins to explain an alternative route to the solution. I immediately become stressed, unable to follow his explanation. I can't think clearly on my feet and I panic. I dismiss class early, turn off the lights, pull down the shades, close and lock the doors, lay my head on my desk and weep.

A few days later, at the doctor's office with Larry, who was getting a routine checkup, I confess to the doctor. "I think I might have Alzheimer's."

"Oh no," he says. "You don't present as having Alzheimer's at all. I don't see that in you."

"OK. Would you like to hear me read?" I ask.

He looks at me doubtfully, likely wondering what I am talking about.

"You see, I have a master's degree in education and have always been a voracious reader, but I seem to be having some difficulty. Go ahead, give me something to read. Anything."

He hands me a pamphlet and I concentrate hard on the words, trying to make sense of them. Pointing to the letters and sounding out the words little by little.

Without the doctor realizing how I might feel, he blurts out, "Oh no, something is terribly wrong."

He seems flustered and confused, not knowing what direction to point me in. Sensing his discomfort, I attempt to shake it off, saying, "Well, thanks for listening. It's good to hear that you don't think it's Alzheimer's. I'll keep trying to figure out what's going on."

I opt to retire early as my reading skills continue to plummet.

From the time I'd returned home from the hospital with my babes in tow, I had been urged to someday write a book about our adventures. Perhaps this is the time, I think, before I lose my reading and writing abilities altogether.

After a year of interviewing the many, many people who are part of our story, I begin the task of organizing the notes I've written down during the interviews. Here is where I run into a snag. I cannot even read my own writing. I am set back, but not utterly defeated. I come up with a new plan that works. Holding my audio recorder close to my Microsoft Word device, I record sections little by little, stopping to listen back for errors in the transcription.

Better get started now rather than later, I muse. This could be a very long process. It seems I can neither keep track of the cursor on the page nor what page I'm on. I end up writing in blocks of two to three lines maximum, followed by an open space of two lines.

Strange, I think, *my expressive language is intact, both written and spoken. But my reading skills are minuscule by comparison.*

Meanwhile, I've started on a battery of psychological tests. But I'm in no hurry, fearful of what the test results might reveal. A process that might have spanned a couple of months stretches out to more than a year.

One Tuesday morning I get a call from the psych department. It's a nurse, not the psychiatrist herself, but she's assigned to report my findings.

"Mrs. Wagner, I have good news. You do not have Alzheimer's. Have you ever taken a fall to your head?" she asks.

And there it is! The culprit. My mind takes me back to that day on the tennis courts when I balked so decisively against the suggestion that I should see a doctor after my fall. I stubbornly insisted that all was well and that there was no cause for alarm.

When I come in to see the neurologist again, she shows me the PET scan that indicates I'd experienced a traumatic brain injury in the left occipital lobe, the language center, which on rare occasions can cause loss of reading/writing skills in adults.

Over the next couple of years, I employ many, many work-arounds in an effort to get this story told. There were frustrations. There were tears and there were triumphs, but the job got done, and here it is—the book you are holding in your hands.

Here and Now

Chad Wagner is a software engineer, but reports that he is first and foremost a father, surfer, cyclist, and climber.

Ben Wagner is a partner in an Am Law 50 law firm where he specializes in intellectual property. Ben enjoys spending time with his family and being outdoors.

Kyle Wagner is an International Educational Consultant who helps forward-thinking schools build more emotionally and globally aware citizens through project-based learning. Currently, he resides in Hong Kong, and spends his free time writing music, traveling, and playing soccer.

Brett Wagner lives in Point Loma, California, with his soul mate/wife of fifteen years, Sarah. They have two beautiful daughters, two dogs, and three chickens. Together, Brett and Sarah run Wagner's School of Music's three San Diego locations. Brett recently released his third studio album, *Waltzes & Poundings*, and spends most of his free time with his family and surfing.

Larry Wagner continues to write music curriculum and original faith-based music, which can be found on spotify.com.

Janna Wagner. I continue to devote myself to three hours of literacy practice daily. The progress is barely perceptible, but is progress nonetheless. When I get discouraged, I refer back to the scripture "He who began a good work in you will be faithful to complete it" (Philippians 1:6). Larry and I begin each day with a devotional over a cup of coffee. We continue to play tennis. We also keep up our flute and piano skills.

Go to www.MagWagPress.com to find color photos of the quads as they grew as well as news stories and video clips.

Acknowledgments

First, I must thank my husband, Larry. His unwavering confidence in my ability to complete the task before me kept me moving forward in my writing. He tolerated countless episodes of my frustrations with technology.

He even tolerated my calls of distress from my perch in my writing loft, all the way across the house:

"Don't worry, Jan, computers can be frustrating. It happens to everyone. Hold tight, I'll be there in three minutes."

"But I just lost ten pages." I'd moan, the tears forming in the corner of my eyes yet again.

"We'll find them, you'll see. Hang on just another minute, can you? I want to finish laying down this piano track. Don't panic."

This rhythm continued over a span of some three years as I did in fact finish what I had begun. But I was not alone, not for a moment. My Jesus and my Larry got me to the finish line.

I will remain eternally grateful for the never-wavering votes of confidence I received from my precious husband throughout the process. Thank you, Larry, for being strong and confident in times when I was not.

There are so many other people who have come alongside our family, who provided support, love, and encouragement, gifts of time and resources, and moments of joy and humor. To list each name would fill a book, but each one has made a difference in our lives, and we are eternally grateful.

We couldn't have done it without folks like you.